THE MYTHS & RELIGION OF
THE INCAS

THE MYTHS & RELIGION OF
THE INCAS

An illustrated encyclopedia of the gods, myths and legends of the
first peoples of South America with over 200 fine-art illustrations

DAVID M JONES

southwater

This edition is published by Southwater,
an imprint of Anness Publishing Ltd
Hermes House, 88–89 Blackfriars Road
London SE1 8HA
tel. 020 7401 2077; fax 020 7633 9499

www.southwaterbooks.com
www.annesspublishing.com

Anness Publishing has a new picture agency
outlet for images for publishing, promotions
or advertising. Please visit our website
www.practicalpictures.com for more information.

UK agent: The Manning Partnership Ltd
tel. 01225 478444; fax 01225 478440
sales@manning-partnership.co.uk

UK distributor: Grantham Book Services Ltd
tel. 01476 541080; fax 01476 541061
orders@gbs.tbs-ltd.co.uk

North American agent/distributor:
National Book Network
tel. 301 459 3366; fax 301 429 5746
www.nbnbooks.com

Australian agent/distributor:
Pan Macmillan Australia
tel. 1300 135 113; fax 1300 135 103
customer.service@macmillan.com.au

New Zealand agent/distributor:
David Bateman Ltd
tel. (09) 415 7664; fax (09) 415 8892

Publisher: Joanna Lorenz
Editor: Joy Wotton
Designers: Nigel Partridge and Adelle Morris
Illustrators: Anthony Duke, Rob Highton
 and Vanessa Card
Editorial Reader: Lindsay Zamponi
Production Controller: Claire Rae

ETHICAL TRADING POLICY
At Anness Publishing we believe that business
should be conducted in an ethical and ecologically
sustainable way, with respect for the environment and a proper regard to the replacement of
the natural resources we employ.

As a publisher, we use a lot of wood pulp to
make high-quality paper for printing, and that
wood commonly comes from spruce trees.
We are therefore currently growing more than
750,000 trees in three Scottish forest plantations:
Berrymoss (130 hectares/320 acres), West
Touxhill (125 hectares/305 acres) and

Deveron Forest (75 hectares/185 acres).
The forests we manage contain more than 3.5
times the number of trees employed each year
in making paper for the books we manufacture.

Because of this ongoing ecological investment
programme, you, as our customer, can have the
pleasure and reassurance of knowing that a
tree is being cultivated on your behalf to naturally replace the materials used to make the
book you are holding.

Our forestry programme is run in accordance
with the UK Woodland Assurance Scheme
(UKWAS) and will be certified by the
internationally recognized Forest Stewardship
Council (FSC). The FSC is a non-government
organization dedicated to promoting responsible
management of the world's forests. Certification
ensures forests are managed in an environmen-
tally sustainable and socially responsible way.
For further information about this scheme, go to
www.annesspublishing.com/trees

© Anness Publishing Ltd 2008

PICTURE ACKNOWLEDGEMENTS
The Ancient Art and Architecture Collection:
5.5, 6bl, 29tr, 36bl, 37bl, 39tl, 67tr, 90–1, 92tr,
99bl, 104tr.

The Art Archive: /Album/J. Enrique
Molina: 80, 95t, 100bl, 109tr, /Amano
Museum, Lima/Album/J. Enrique Molina:
110bl, /Amano Museum, Lima/Dagli Orti:
5br, 21tm, /Amano Museum, Lima/Mireille
Vautier: 17bl, 100tr, /Archaeological
Museum, Lima/Album/J. Enrique Molina:
96bl, /Archaeological Museum, Lima/Dagli
Orti: 12bl, 18bl, 18tr, 23bm, 30bl, 55tr,
55bm, 56, 64bl, 93br, 105, 106bl, 120tr,
/Archaeological Museum, Lima/Mireille
Vautier: 35bl, 79tr, 110tr, 122bl,
/Archbishops Palace Museum, Cuzco/
Mireille Vautier: 86tl, /Arteaga Collection,
Peru/Mireille Vautier: 27br, 86br,
/Bibliothèque des Arts Décoratifs, Paris
/Dagli Orti: 114bl, /Stephanie Colasanti:
36tr, 41tr, 45t, 87tm, 87br, 115tl, 120bl,
/Dagli Orti: 4.4, 4.5, 5.1, 8–9, 13bl, 20tr,
26, 38bl, 38br, 42bl, 42tr, 45br, 46bl, 47bl,
48tl, 52tr, 53t, 54bl, 66, 68bl, 69bl, 71t,

76tr, 89br, 96tr, 118tr, /Chavez Ballon
Collection, Lima/Mireille Vautier:
70tr, /Gold Museum, Lima/Mireille Vautier:
61, /Money Museum, Potosi, Bolivia/Mireille
Vautier: 117tr, /Museo Banco de Guayaquil,
Ecuador/Dagli Orti: 5.3, 50–1, /Museo de
Arte Colonial de Santa Catalina, Cuzco/Dagli
Orti: 116, /Museo de Arte Municipal,
Lima/Dagli Orti: 107, /Museo del Banco
Central de Reserva, Lima/Dagli Orti: 111bl,
/Museo del Oro, Lima/Dagli Orti: 17tr, 97,
103br, 104bl, /Museo Nacional de Historica,
Lima/Mireille Vautier: 125tr, /Museo Pedro de
Osma, Lima/Dagli Orti: 5.6, 112–13, /Museo
Pedro de Osma, Lima/Mireille Vautier: 84tr,
85bl, /Museo Regional de Ica, Peru/Dagli Orti:
59, /Museum Larco Herra, Lima/Album/J.
Enrique Molina: 54tm, /University Museum,
Cuzco/Mireille Vautier: 34bl, 35tr, 52bl,
/Mireille Vautier: 103tl, 114tr, 123bl.

Andrew McLeod: 16tm, 37tr, 126tm, 128br, 128tr.

Sally Phillips: 34tr.

Frances Reynolds: 126br.

Nick Saunders: 23tr, 32tr, 38tr, 40bl, 47tr,
49br, 62, 70bl, 74bl, 84bl, 98t, 101, 111tl,
117bl, 121.

South American Pictures: 68tr, 74tr, 75bl,
81bl, 95br, 102tr, 106tr, 109bl, 115br, 126bl,
127tm /Jason P. Howe: 124tr, /Kathy Jarvis:
4.2, 4.3, 19tr, 21br, /Kimball Morrison: 53br,
/Marion Morrison: 76bl, /Tony Morrison: 1, 2,
4br, 4.1, 5.4, 6tr, 7tl, 10bl, 10tr, 11tr, 12tr, 14,
16b, 20bl, 22bl, 32bl, 33tl, 33br, 39br, 40tr,
41bl, 43tr, 43bl, 46tr, 49tl, 54br, 57b, 58bl,
60bl, 64tr, 67bl, 71bm, 72–3, 75tr, 77t, 78bl,
78tr, 79bl, 81tr, 82bl, 82tr, 83bl, 83tr, 88bl,
89tl, 92bl, 93tl, 98bm, 118bl, 119br, 122tr,
123tr, 124bl, 125bl, /Kim Richardson: 119t,
119bl, /Chris Sharp: 7br, 94tr.

Werner Forman Archive: 13tr, 15tl, /British
Museum, London: 15br, 30tr, / Dallas Museum
of Art, Dallas: 3, 11bl, 99tr, /David Bernstein
Collection, New York: 4.6, 22r, 28tr, 58tr,
/Museum für Völkerkunde, Berlin: 29bl,
63bl, 65tl, 65br, 77bl, 94bl, 102bl, 108,
111br, /Private Collection: 5.2, 24–5, 29br,
31bl, /Royal Museum of Art & History,
Brussels: 60tr.

p.1 Carved Inca face.
*p. 2 Winay Wayna, on the hillside above
the Urubamba River.*
p.3 Moche effigy jar.

CONTENTS

INTRODUCTION

Religious beliefs and deities were intimately linked with the forces of nature. Ancient South American peoples felt compelled to explain the important things in their universe, beginning with where they came from and their place in the larger scheme of things. To do this they developed accounts of what they could see in the sky and in the surrounding landscape to help them understand which things were important, and how and why this was so. Thus, the Inca god Inti belonged to the life-giving force of the sun, and Lake Titicaca, the most sacred of waters, was seen as the origin of life.

The explanatory accounts of these concepts provided a framework for living and for understanding and relating to the mysteries of the world.

The legends and myths of the Andean peoples, together with the remains found by archaeologists, constitute a record of ancient Andean religious belief.

COMMON BELIEFS AND IMAGERY

There were long sequences of traditional development among Andean and western coastal peoples and cultures. Many deities were almost universal, although given different names by different cultures, but some were individual and distinct, belonging to particular peoples and civilizations.

Nevertheless, long-standing places of ritual pilgrimage linked areas and regions and persisted despite the rise and fall of

kingdoms and empires. The site and oracle of coastal Pachacamac, for example, had such potency and precedence that even the Incas recognized and revered it, although they felt compelled to establish their imperial authority by building a temple to the sun god Inti in its shadow.

Common threads run through the mythologies of Andean Area civilization and its cultures. Today's modern division of religion and politics was unknown then, at a time when the entire basis of political power was derived from divine development and designation. In Inca

Left: Gold hammered sheet-metal sun figure from Tiwanaku. The rayed head is reminiscent of the Gateway of the Sun.

Above: Cotton-embroidered textile from the Early Horizon Paracas culture, with a figure reminiscent of the Chavín Staff Deity.

society, and probably in Chimú and Moche and other cultures before them, rulers and priests were often one and the same. The Inca ruler himself was regarded as the living divine representative of Inti. Although each had specific roles, rulers and priests were intimately entwined in ruling and regulating every aspect of daily life. Ruler worship was carried beyond death through continuing ritual with the mummies of past Incas.

The landscape itself was considered sacred. Numerous natural features were regarded as semi-divine; ceremonial centres

were constructed to represent myth; and ritual pathways were made across long distances, such as Nazca geoglyphic or Inca *ceque* routes.

There were many common religious elements among ancient Andean cultures, some of them almost universal, some more regional. In most regions, for example, there was a named creator god. During the later stages of Andean civilization – the Late Intermediate Period and Late Horizon – Viracocha, with many variations, was the creator god, especially among the sierra cultures and many coastal cultures. Along the central and southern Peruvian coast there was also a certain confusion and/or rivalry with the supreme god Pachacamac. Prototypes of the creator god Viracocha are apparent in the architectural and artistic imagery of earlier civilizations.

Religious imagery throughout the Andean Area was profoundly influenced from the earliest times by rainforest animals (most notably jaguars, but also serpents and other reptiles, monkeys, birds) and included composite humanoid beings. Among symbolic motifs that persisted through the different cultures of the Andean Area, in addition to the jaguar, were feline-human hybrids, staff deities (often with a composite feline face and human body), winged beings, and falcon- or other bird-headed warriors.

Left: Nazca geoglyph forming a monkey in the desert of southern Peru. Such animals figure frequently in desert coastal cultures.

ANDEAN THEMES

Several common themes pervade Andean Area religion. As well as the creator Viracocha, almost all ritual had a calendrical organization. There was a calendar based on the movements of heavenly bodies, including solar solstices and equinoxes, lunar phases, the synodical cycle of Venus, the rising and setting of the Pleiades, the rotational inclinations of the Milky Way and the presence within the Milky Way of 'dark cloud constellations' (stellar voids).

Consultation of auguries concerning these movements was considered vital at momentous times of the year, including planting, the harvest and the start of the ocean fishing season.

Sacrifice, both human and animal, and a variety of offerings were other common practices. An extremely important and ancient theme was the assignment of sacredness to special places, called *huacas*. The use of hallucinogenic and other drugs was widespread, especially coca and the buds of several cacti, in rituals connected to war and sacrifice. Another common practice was ancestor reverence and worship. The mummified remains of ancestors were kept in special chambers, or in caves, and brought out on ritual occasions.

It is this diversity, imaginative invention and richness of expression and depiction, as well as its 'alien' appeal – at least to Western readers – that makes the religion/mythology of Andean civilization so fascinating.

Below: Chinchorros mummies, c.5000BC, in the Atacama Desert are the world's earliest known deliberate mummifications.

CHAPTER ONE

A PANTHEON OF GODS

Sanctity permeated the ancient Andean world. Sacred powers were everywhere, in all living things. Survival in this world, the land of the living, was dependent not only on producing enough to eat, but also on revering the gods and appeasing them through rituals, sacrifices and offerings. At the same time, there was a fatalism in the belief in the great cycle of being, of life and death, which gave rise to the reverence of ancestors.

The peoples of the Andean Area held a range of beliefs and appear to have worshipped a pantheon of deities with control over different aspects of nature. Their religious beliefs developed from the earliest times, and they can be detected in the architecture and art of the earliest Andean civilizations. Many deities were universally accepted throughout the Andean Area, sometimes called by different names but having the same essential attributes, powers and roles.

A linking factor throughout Andean life was that of continuity, of how all things are connected and so part of a cycle, and this was demonstrated through the concepts of mutual exchange, duality and collectivity, which were all vital parts of spiritual and daily life for ancient Andeans. Continuity was intensely developed in Andean civilization through the pilgrimage centres, such as Chavín de Huántar and Pachacamac, that persisted over centuries and endured despite political rivalry and changing political developments.

Left: The central figure of the Gateway of the Sun, at Tiwanaku, is a ray-encircled face in the pose of the Chavín Staff Deity.

THEMES AND BELIEFS

The long sequence of development among Andean highland and lowland peoples fostered mutually beneficial relationships between cultures. Constant contact between regions brought the exchange of ideas as well as produce and commodities.

ANDEAN THEMES

Through Andean history, common themes were expressed in art and architecture. Coastal animals and motifs were copied in highland traditions and vice versa.

The early combination of temple platforms and sunken courts shows this exchange of ideas in the architectural elements of the ceremonial centre. Platforms mimic mountain peaks and plateaux, while sunken courts mimic valleys and coastal desert oases. It can be argued that ritual progression through such ceremonial complexes reflects the symbiotic relationship between highland

Below: Part of the outcrop of the sacred Inca huaca *at Qenqo, north of Cuzco, was believed to be a giant seated puma turned to stone.*

Right: An Early Intermediate Period Nazca bridge-spouted pot depicts the Oculate Being accompanied by trophy heads.

and lowland cultures and between mountain and coastal deities.

This architectural combination also shows the early appearance of the Andean concept of duality. The late Preceramic Period union of platform mound and sunken court, both in highland and lowland sites, constituted the first widespread Andean 'religion'. To agricultural peoples, the sunken court was probably the focus for the worship of 'mother earth' – for the ritual re-enactment of birth or creation represented by spring crops. The ascent of the platform may have been the recognition of the upper world in which the god of creation dwelled, or from which came the waters that made agriculture possible.

The highland site of Chavín de Huántar not only combined the elements of platform and sunken court, but also introduced the idea of a sacred location widely accepted as the focus of worship for peoples throughout the central Andes and coast. The Chavín Cult developed the labyrinthine temple complex within which cult statuary was secreted, with all its obscure meaning, perhaps interpretable only by shamans.

With the development of the Chavín cult also came religious art expressing duality and a prototype supreme creator god, forerunner to representations of Viracocha in later Andean civilizations. The Staff Deity, significantly represented both as male and female, was an undisguised representation of duality. In varying forms, a deity holding staffs with outstretched arms was an artistic motif from Chavín to Inca times. In the courtyard of Chavín de Huántar's New Temple stood the 0.5m (1½ft) stone sculpture of the supreme deity. Holding a *Strombus* shell in one hand and a *Spondylus* shell in the other, the deity also manifested duality, as a metaphor for the balancing of male and female forces in the universe, and the union of opposing forces, providing completion through unity.

COMMON BELIEFS

Thus, despite variations in regional and cultural detail, the earliest ceremonial centres reflect common elements of belief.

The continuing highland–lowland interchange was cemented in the recognition of certain ceremonial centres as places of pilgrimage, Chavín de Huántar being the first. Platforms with sunken courtyards and pilgrimage centres were elements of Andean civilization for 2,500 years. Pilgrimage centres were recognized by both highland and coastal states, linking regions and persisting through political change. The cult centre of Chavín de Huántar endured for more than 500 years, while the site and oracle of coastal Pachacamac, beginning in the 1st century AD, lasted more than a millennium.

The Incas had a complex calendar of worship based on the movements of heavenly bodies, including solar solstices

Below: A Late Intermediate Period Chimú mummy bundle with a copper burial mask, painted red, feather headdress and two flutes.

Above: An Early Intermediate Period Nazca sheet-gold burial mask. A burial with such a mask indicates high-status.

and equinoxes, lunar phases, the synodic cycle of Venus, the rising and setting of the Pleiades, the rotational inclinations of the Milky Way, and the presence within the Milky Way of 'dark cloud constellations' (stellar voids). Consultation of auguries concerning these movements was vital at momentous times of the year, such as planting time, harvest time and the beginning of the ocean fishing season. Inca practices represent the final stage of the development of such beliefs.

Sacrifice, both human and animal, and a variety of offerings were common. Ritual strangulation and beheading are well attested in burials and art such as ceramic painting, murals, architectural sculpture, textiles and metalwork.

As well as pilgrimage sites, tens of thousands of places – *huacas* – were held sacred. Like pilgrimage centres, their importance could endure for centuries. *Huacas* could be springs (emphasizing the importance of water), caves (prominent in human origin mythology), mountains, rocks or stones, fields or towns where important events had taken place, lakes or islands in them, or man-made objects

such as stone pillars erected at specific locations.

Shrines and temples were sometimes built at *huacas*, but just as often the object/place was left in its natural state.

The ritual use of hallucinogenic drugs was widespread. Coca (*Erythroxylon coca*) leaves were chewed in a complex and multi-stage ritual connected with war and sacrifice. Cactus buds and hallucinogenic mushrooms were also used.

The reverence for ancestors is evident in the special treatment of mummified burials in the Chinchorros culture of northern coastal Chile. Such practice developed into ancestor worship and became charged with special ritual, governed by the cyclical calendar by Inca times. Mummified remains of ancestors were carefully kept in special buildings, rooms or chambers, or in caves, and were themselves considered *huacas*. They were brought out on ritual occasions to participate in the festivals and to be offered delicacies of food and drink, as well as objects and prayers.

Preoccupation with death included the underworld. Skeletal figures, depictions of priests imitating the dead to visit the underworld, and skeletal figures with sexual organs or the dead embracing women were associated with fertility beliefs and the source of life in the underworld.

PACHACUTI – THE ENDLESS CYCLE

To the ancient Andeans everything around them, in all directions, was sacred. They believed themselves to be in a universe that was forever in cycle, *pachacuti*, in an endless revolution of time and history. The concept of *pachacuti* is further revealed in the Andean belief that humankind went through several phases of creation, destruction and re-creation. This progression was held to reflect the gods' desire to create an increasingly perfected form of humans. Honour and worship of the gods was so important that it took several efforts to create beings of proper humility. This veneration was essential because it was 'known' that at the slightest provocation they were capable of destroying the world.

A DIVIDED UNIVERSE

The ancient Andeans' universe comprised three levels: the world of the living, which the Incas called Kai Pacha, the world below, called Uku Pacha, and the world of the heavens, called Hanan Pacha. Kai Pacha comprised the relatively flat surface of the earth and lay between the other two. As the world of humans, Kai Pacha was also called Hurin Pacha – lower world.

Above: Warrior figures on this Paracas burial textile, c.500BC, are shown in the symbolic pose of the Chavín Staff Deity.

As well as this vertical arrangement, the Inca universe was divided by two horizontal axes running through the points of the compass. The centre of both realms ran through Cuzco, where the vertical axis of the three realms and the horizontal axes intersected.

Pervading the entire universe was the creator god – the all-powerful, "formless" one – Viracocha (as the Inca and many others knew him).

AN ECOLOGICAL RELATIONSHIP

The relationship maintained between ancient Andeans and their universe can be characterized as 'ecological'. Because they perceived their environment as sacred, they believed that they were on earth not to exploit it but rather to enjoy its benefits through the grace of the gods. The relationship was one of deity power and human supplication. Humans considered themselves to be not the centre or focus of the world but only one group among all living things – including animals, plants and the stars. Thus humans appealed to the gods for their permission to make use of the various other elements of the world. Indeed, the animals, plants and stars were rather more important than humans, for it was in them that the gods were personified.

Left: Long-distance trade contacts also spread imagery. Here a rainforest monkey decorates a coastal desert Nazca ceramic vessel.

Right: An Inca textile showing a deity or a shaman, impersonating a god with sky-snake image and the stance of the Staff Deity.

AN EVOLVING RELIGION

More is known about Inca beliefs than other beliefs of the Andean Area because they were formed into an official state religion and cult of the emperor, Inti, as the earthly representative of the sun. Inca religion itself was the final stage in a long sequence of development from primitive beliefs. Inca conquest brought their people into contact with many other cultures and regions, each of which also had its own religious development.

Upon conquest, Spanish clergy and administrators recorded Inca beliefs and concepts in their attempts to understand more about the peoples of the empire. Archaeologists believed that the concepts and physical remains of Inca religion can be projected into the pre-Inca past. They also detect many common themes in ancient Andean development because the archaeological evidence indicates that pre-Inca deities, whose names are mostly unknown, nevertheless represented the same or very similar concepts to those of Inca dcities.

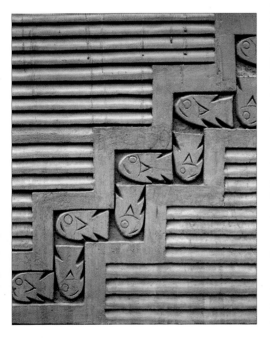

FUNDAMENTAL DUALITY

Following the fundamental Andean belief in duality, the universe and everything in it comprised two parts in opposition, but striving for completion through unity, thus male/female, light/dark, hot/cold, good/evil, the sun/the moon.

To civilizations based primarily on agriculture for their day-to-day existence, the natural world and its physical forces represented essential elements of survival. The natural elements were considered divine and ruled human existence as evidence of the gods' powers. Ancient Andeans naturally sought to give the

Left: Fish, perhaps in a river channel, decorate the sculpted compound mud walls at the Chimú capital of Chan Chan.

deities and their powers 'forms' in representational art and architecture, and common themes can be detected from at least the Initial Period in its ceremonial architecture. A pantheon of deities and beliefs is evident from at least Chavín times in the Early Horizon.

The Andean pantheon in its entirety was extremely complex and varied throughout the regions. Almost universal, however, was the belief in a creator god, known as Viracocha in the highland and inland regions and Pachacmac among Pacific coastal cultures. In addition, the sun and the moon were deities called by numerous names in different cultures and through time. Usually, but not always, the sun was regarded as male and the moon as female.

TRANSFORMATION

Ancient Americans throughout the North and South American continents believed that the universe existed on multiple levels. The Inca tripartite realms of the living world, a world above and a world below were the culmination of developments from the beginning of Andean religion. The realms were not held to be exclusive, nor were they necessarily separated in time. Rather, they existed in parallel, and each was vital to the existence of the other two.

Communication between these worlds was achieved through transformation. Birth, living and death were therefore considered states of existence in an endlessly continuing cycle of time, rather than as mutually exclusive states. Each realm could influence the others, and actions in the realm of the living could influence the effects of the other realms on it. Thus, it was important to maintain communications between the realms by worshipping the gods and by honouring one's ancestors, who were believed to be 'living' in the realm of the dead. Shamanism provided the medium that enabled communication between worlds, and it was through shamans or 'priests' that instructive and corrective messages could be obtained in the world of the living.

A BALANCED ORDER

The world was ordered according to specific rules that governed how things should be and how they should work. Social and economic order had to be upheld in order to maintain the balance between the worlds.

Right: This Sipán sheet-gold burial mask represents various Andean themes: the sun and the shamanic transformation or human representation of a deity.

As with reciprocity and collectivity, equal power among individuals was not required, only that all were included within the scheme and received sufficient necessities. In this way, social and economic functions can be seen as constant factors within the different political systems that evolved over time in the Andean Area. For example, the architecture of ceremonial centres, from the early U-shaped structures and sunken courts of the Initial Period, through to Chavín temples in the Early Horizon to Late Horizon Inca state religion, continued the theme of dualism, as did the practice of the collection and redistribution of goods and divisions of labour, despite the rise and fall of kingdoms and empires.

STATES OF CHANGE

The universe was considered to be in a state of flux, but its changes were cyclical and orderly. The seasons changed in regular succession, the climate altered between wet to dry seasons. Moisture was collected into and channelled by earthly rivers, taken up into the celestial river, and fell back to earth as rain and snow in a never-ending redistributive cycle. Planting, harvest, storage and redistribution formed an endless cycle. The movements of the sun, moon, planets and stars were observed to be regular, as was the progression of the Milky Way through the night sky. Thus, orderly regularity governed all realms.

Likewise, individual lives were in states of flux, from birth to youth to old age, and continued in death as the next plane of existence.

Such cyclical thinking was (and continues to be) the key to the Andean worldview. Human history progresses but is perceived to repeat itself constantly. For example, the Incas saw in the ruins of Tiwanaku a former earthly kingdom that preceded their own and thought of themselves as the inheritors of Tiwanaku power in the Altiplano.

HUMAN TO SUPERNATURAL

Andean art served to reflect these planes of existence and to unite them. It captured transformations such as the metamorphosis of shamans into supernatural beings. Artists strove to develop methods and media to depict the world as dynamic and to show two things as one, or the existence of a shaman beyond terrestrial space. Transformational examples can be seen in the statuary of Initial

14

Above: The transfixed stare of this effigy figurine represents a shaman under the influence of hallucinogenic drugs, a frequent theme in Moche ceramic art.

Right: A deer-headed human-like ceramic figurine, representing the completed transformation of a shaman into a revered animal. His headdress bears a knife for ritual sacrifice.

impersonating and transforming into animals – subjects of this world as representations of the superhuman world. Likewise, the importance of communication between realms is clearly shown in numerous Moche ceramics depicting shamanistc acts, and in the inclusion of Inca mummies in the annual ritual cycle.

Finally, Inca religious narrative abounds in examples of transformations: ancestors to stone, animals to stone, humans /deities to stone, humans to animals, and stones to supernatural warriors. Early Cuzco itself owes its survival to 'stones transformed into warriors'.

Period sites such as Huaca de los Reyes, in the fibre human effigies at Mina Perdida and in the painted adobe sculptures at Moxeke. The composite features of these beings, which were represented by non-human eyes with pendent irises, feline noses, fangs, drawn-back lips and facial scarifications, and condor markings on the Mina Perdida fibre effigy, are all indicative of human transformation. Such elements heavily influenced the Chavín style of the Early Horizon in jaguar and serpentine animal–human transformers. The Staff Being him/herself carries all these elements, as do the various monumental stone sculptures of Chavín, especially the more than 40 sculptures, stone heads and relief panels on the walls of the New Temple, showing a time-lapse sequence of human to supernatural transformation from shaman to feline.

The care with which Paracas and Nazca burials were wrapped and preserved, the sumptuous burials of Moche and Sicán lords and the ritual preservation of Chimú and Inca rulers are all indicative of the importance of transformation between states of being. Many Paracas and Nazca textiles depict humans ritually

A UNITED WORLDVIEW

Essence is a fundamental concept or theme in ancient Andean belief and artistic expression. Essence united the Andean peoples' worldview, incorporating reciprocity/duality, collectivity and transformation. It expressed their belief that the core element or underlying substance was more important than appearance.

REALITY AND MEANING

The symbol of an object represented its reality, even if it was hidden by its outward appearance. It was not important for an image to be visible, or for the material of an object to be pure, for its essence was still present and governed belief. Objects were created for their own sakes and in this sense de-humanized. Such lack of emphasis on the importance

Above: Beneath the stonework of the Machu Picchu Observatorio lies a ritual room made with minimal sculpting of the natural rock.

Below: The essence of gold is conveyed through the gilding of less precious copper and silver in this Moche Sipán funeral mask.

of the human audience underscores Andean regard for humans as only one part of the universe in their worldview. Even the depiction of humans in ancient Andean art was not necessarily the most important component. With the exception of Moche art, there was little individualism or recognition of people. Individuals normally played a part in the whole and are subservient to the theme of the work.

Symbolism was far more important. It was used to convey the idea and to represent the thought or the character of a deity or of a scene. The idea was to characterize someone or something through the use of recognizable traits commonly known and spread with the movement of religious cults.

ESSENCE IN ART

A large part of artistic production was not created for daily use but was made for its own sake by craftworkers, and by artists who were subsidized by the political elite. Thus, Andean potters used moulds to make hundreds, if not thousands, of identical pieces representing aspects of Andean life and religion. Metallurgists would mask a base or less precious core with a more precious metal, or gild objects made of alloys. Architectural sculpture emphasized interior decoration and symbolic representation of deities and sacred acts. Elaborate, rich burials were filled with products made solely to be included in the burial. Textile weavers executed such elaborate patterns that the subject often became illegible but was still true to the supernatural subject.

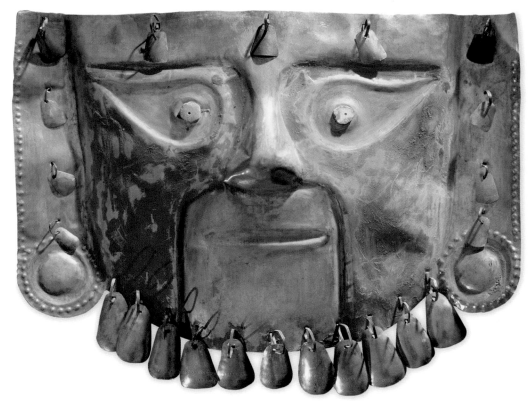

Essence explains why it was not necessary for the Nazca geoglyphs and other ground drawings to be seen in their entirety: it was quite acceptable that the ritual pathways they prescribed could be followed and that the lines fulfilled their function in religious devotion. Thus, their essence was conveyed in the doing rather than in the seeing.

Similar reasoning may explain the use of openwork weaving in Late Intermediate Period Chancay textiles. The designs could be seen as the weaver worked them on the loom, creating interlocking animals and birds, but once removed from the loom the threads contracted and their symbolic imagery became illegible when the garment was worn. Only when spread out against a dark background could the imagery be appreciated – an example of the value of essence over appearance.

Likewise, sacred images were often placed in obscure or hidden locations within temples. The meaning and essence was conveyed to the people by shamans, sometimes personifying the deity concerned, sometimes rep-

Above: Traces of red paint on this sheet-gold Chimú funerary mask show that its essence (pure gold) was hidden in a reverse of the idea represented by gilding (see opposite).

resenting the deity through transformation. Similarly, the symbolic images could be so complex, or arranged so strangely over a stone or a pot, as to render them accessible only to an elite few. For it was what the images stood for that was important rather than that all should be able to stand before them and 'read' their intimate meaning.

Most artistic production was created for its own sake, for the afterlife, for its ritual efficacy or for use within the realm of the supernatural.

RHYTHM AND ENERGY

Reciprocity, collectivity, transformation and essence facilitated the rhythms of ancient Andean life. Their interconnections guided the flow of the world and manifested the Inca concept of *ayni*, the principle that governed cyclicity. In the words of one scholar, reciprocity was 'like a pump at the heart of Andean life'. Together these concepts represent the energy that bound the cycle of the universe, the *ayni* and *mink'a* – the positive and negative, the give and take that made the Andean universe work.

Left: Moche red-on-white 'story' vessels depicted common activities as well as ritual: here a fisherman uses a pelican to fish.

MULTIPLE MEANINGS IN ART

Art often elicits dual meanings, inviting opposite or multiple interpretations. Such double readings are common in Andean art. Textiles from the earliest times right through to Chancay and Inca weaving in the Late Horizon dovetail mirror images of birds and animals. Two-headed supernatural creatures are shown in textiles, painted decoration and sculpture. Inca architecture plays with opposites, 'sculpting' natural stone to display light and shadow. Beings, real and supernatural, with double meanings, portrayed as a single motif with multiple identities abound in Early Horizon Chavín and Paracas art and continue through the ages in the art of later highland and coastal cultures.

Below: The shape of this Nazca effigy vessel makes it difficult to interpret. The mythological themes on its faces may be individual or may comprise a narrative.

EARLY SYMBOLIC ART

The idea that essential meaning could be depicted visually, and that a representation could contain multiple meanings and show a composite being was present in some of the earliest Andean art. Cotton textiles from Huaca Prieta employed a relatively simple twining technique. More than 9,000 cloth fragments were excavated. The most famous piece, only known as a photographic reproduction, shows a clearly recognizable raptor with a hooked beak and outstretched wings. Closer inspection shows a coiled snake within its stomach. The subject's basic symmetry, broken by its left-facing beak, is balanced by the right-facing slant of the snake.

The embedded serpent reveals a multi-layered meaning. Here is a raptor and its prey. The obvious victory of raptor over snake, however, may represent a religious belief or hierarchy. The zigzag contours of the piece indicate that it was held sideways as it was twined, revealing that the weaver was able to visualize the final design during execution. The use of this method may also have been so that the visual impact of the zigzag was of beating wings. Thus, complexity of meaning and mode of manufacture reveal how essence of meaning was paramount and more important than both simple imagery and method.

Another example of multiple meaning and of the early portrayal of a composite being also comes from Huaca Prieta. A twined cotton fragment shows the symmetrical figure of two crabs in a rhomboidal composition. One crab occupies the lower left and the other the upper right. Outstretched legs indicate that they are scuttling. Curiously, one has eight legs while the other has six. However,

Above: This vessel may depict shamanic transformation or earthly representation for a ritual involving a sky deity. Many Moche effigy vessels contain obscured meaning.

they are not just crabs. The bases of the crabs are united by one pair of their claws across the centre of the composition. Each of the other claws, however, bends in an acute angle back towards the head of the twin crab and turns into a snake's head. The angular representation hints at the nature of the animal. Not only is there double meaning in this piece in the representation of a land and a sea animal, but also the multi-layered meaning of one animal turning into the other. Perhaps the wearer was meant to become infused with the character of the animals.

MEANING WITHIN ARCHITECTURE

At the other end of the Andean chronological scale, the Inca *huaca* of Qenqo, just north of Cuzco, shows the same concepts rendered in architecture and stone sculpture. The natural outcrop has been heavily modified, its protruding surfaces carved extensively with steps, shelves, indentations and niches. There is also a zigzag channel that branches and rejoins, which may have been for libations. Such heavy alteration rivals the outcrops' natural irregularity. It is difficult to decide whether the modifications are meant to mimic, oppose or balance the natural irregularities. The play on light and shadow is carried to the extreme, yet some flat surfaces reflect the sun's rays so fiercely that the 'play' becomes one-sided.

Beneath the huge boulder lies hidden meaning. A large natural cleft has been carved into a small chamber. The natural 'heart' of such a stone was a quintessential Andean place of sacredness, and the modification of it recognized this and rendered it available for ritual purposes. It is the essence of the outcrop that is important; its modification by humans emphasizes and enhances its sacredness. Its use recognizes its vitality.

To ancient Andeans, Qenqo and other such sites were not inanimate objects but living beings, part of the universe. The hidden heart at Qenqo's base isolates it from the secular world; its alteration and use bring it into the spiritual world.

A separate, protruding monolith to one side of the main outcrop is naturally triangular and has been left uncarved.

Above: Eagle and hawk carvings on the columns of the Black and White Portal of the New Temple at Chavín de Huántar.

When viewed from a certain angle, its shape resembles that of a seated puma. It is framed by a small square wall and by an enclosing curved courtyard wall. Once again, the recognition of its shape and use as a place of ritual draws it into the Inca universe. A rainforest creature in this mountain setting unifies the realms of the world.

Left: Rolled-out reconstruction drawings of the female eagle (left) and male hawk (right) carved on the columns at Chavín.

HIDDEN RITUAL AND MEANING

Every form of ancient Andean art contains layers of meaning. Obscuring this meaning within many possible interpretations and in a complex design became fully developed in Early Horizon times at Chavín de Huántar, like so many features of ancient Andean religion. Earlier elements of Chavín religion can be seen in the preceding Preceramic and Initial Periods.

PLATFORM MOUNDS

The architectural tradition of Preceramic platform mound sites began the practice of building small courtyards and chambers or groups of chambers on top of platforms. It is not possible to describe in detail what rituals took place in them, but they were clearly meant to hide whatever activity they enclosed. The platforms' location at the centres of ceremonial complexes and above domestic buildings isolated them, and their relatively small size made them accessible to only a chosen few. The steps leading up to such platforms presumably provided the venue for ritual display to multitudes. In this way, what different groups within society witnessed could be selected and controlled.

The deliberately broken and buried figurines at Huaca de los Idolos at Aspero represent one of the earliest examples of such hidden, selective ritual, as do the infant and adult burial at its companion mound of Huaca de los Sacrificios.

Above: The high, thick compound walls of the Huaca el Dragón, near Chan Chan, enclose the people performing the rituals within them.

The tradition was elaborated in the Initial Period at sites such as La Galgada, Kotosh, Caral and Chiripa. Twinned and multiple mounds were built at many sites, and chambers were either detached but grouped, a tradition that continued through to Inca times, or became combined in complexes divided into rooms. Larger halls were subdivided into separate chambers or divided partially to hide one part within another. Parts of complexes were made difficult to enter through long galleries leading around behind a main complex.

Kotosh, La Galgada, Aspero, Piedra Parada, El Paraíso, Sechín Alto, Cerro Sechín, Huaca de los Reyes, Garagay and numerous other sites went through such transitions. In the Titiucaca Basin, Chiripa shows the emphasis on symmetrically grouped detached chambers built on top of a platform.

HIDDEN PLAZAS

The tradition of hidden plazas (*plazas hundidas*) established an opposing organization of space by enclosing and isolating ritual within negative space. Hidden plazas

Left: The Semi-subterranean Court beyond the Kalasasaya portal at Tiwanaku is an example of a sunken ritual courtyard.

may have been venues for ritual re-enactments of creation and earth veneration. The combination of the two traditions became common at sites in the late Initial Period and Early Horizon and is most elaborately represented at Chavín de Huántar. Hidden plazas were initially circular at northern Andean sites. The transition from circular to rectangular took place at Chavín de Huántar in the 1st millennium BC. Within the arms of the U-shaped platform housing the Old Temple stood the circular sunken court, while the plaza of the New Temple incorporated a square sunken court, and heralded the persistence of the rectangular form in the Altiplano until the demise of Tiwanaku at the end of the 10th century AD.

The objects of worship and the chambers that housed them also became more complicated, hidden and controlled. The labyrinthine chambers of the Old and New Temples at Chavín de Huántar are the classic example. Deep within its galleries and corridors, a dimly lit room in the Old Temple held the Lanzón Stone monolith and in the New Temple stood the Raimondi Stela. A third monolith, the Tello Obelisk, stood in the sunken court of the New Temple.

ORACLES AND IMAGES

The use of oracles at Chavín de Huántar and at Pachacamac represents another aspect of ritual obscurity. Only specialists could interpret the oracles' pronouncements. The supplicant required shamanistic intervention and interpretation. At Chavín de Huántar, the base of the Lanzón Stone stood in the lower chamber, while an upper chamber, into which its top protruded, provided a hidden chamber for the voice of the oracle. The principal idol at Pachacamac was a wooden statue kept in a windowless room at the summit of the main terraced platform.

Above: Detailed scenes or mythical events painted on Nazca pottery must be read carefully to obtain their full meaning.

The symbolic images of the Chavín monoliths and of the Black and White Portal of the New Temple show multiple meaning and obscurity in several ways. All three sculptures depict supernatural beings and include snarling faces. They are three representations of the supreme being, and the features on them are repeated in modified form in Chavín portable art found throughout the central Andes and coast regions in Early Horizon settlements.

The positioning of the images enhances the obscurity of their meaning. They are not only extremely intricate and complex but are also wrapped around the monoliths or columns of the portal and thus cannot be seen all at the same time or in total without walking around the scultpure. The location of the Lanzón Stone makes this impossible. In the Titicaca Basin the Yaya-Mama tradition on monolithic slabs at Pukará and other sites, showing a male (*yaya*) and a female (*mama*) figure on opposite faces, demonstrates a similar principle.

These traditions of isolating and secluding ritual continued to the Late Horizon. The Late Intermediate Chimú capital at Chan Chan comprised a huge complex of individual rectangular complexes. The Inca Coricancha in Cuzco enclosed a group of chambers dedicated to individual deities and secluded ritual for specialized priests, who thus controlled the rare display of venerated objects.

Below: The Circular Sunken Court at Chavín de Huántar brought a coastal ritual feature to the mountain cult.

SYMBOLS OF DIVINITY

The integrated nature of the ancient Andean worldview regarded natural objects as sacred. Mountains, water and caves were universal divine symbols. Within ancient Andean belief there was an intentional melding of what modern Western cultures regard as natural and cultural; both were regarded as 'living'.

SUN AND MOON

Tracking the cycles of the sun and moon is important to agricultural peoples, and the ancient Andeans were no exception. The sun, Ai Apaec (Moche and Chimú) or Inti (Inca), and the moon, Si (Moche and Chimú) or Quilla (Inca), were universal symbols of reverence and were believed to exercise enormous influence on human life. They were associated with precious metals: gold with the sun, silver with the moon. The association became a physical metaphor to the Incas: sweat of the sun

Below: The cult of Inti, the Inca sun god, centred on Intihuatana (Hitching Post of the Sun) sites, such as this one at Machu Picchu.

and tears of the moon. Most cultures considered the moon to be the consort of the sun. They symbolized opposing forces, and their intermingled cycles achieved the unity necessary to the world's balance. Their controlled cycles gave stability to the pre-Hispanic world.

The Incas epitomized the importance of the sun in their state cult, in which the emperor was the sun's earthly representative – son of the sun. The Incas regarded themselves as the children of the sun and moon, and in the creation myth Viracocha, the creator god, is also described as the sun.

The sun is not easily identified in pre-Hispanic art. Gold generally symbolizes it, but a specific solar deity is not obvious. Inca gold-rayed masks clearly represent the sun, and the god in the centre of the lintel of the stone portal at Tiwanaku may represent the sun, hence its name Gateway of the Sun.

The moon was intimately related to earthly matters. Images of a crescent moon feature especially in pre-Inca Moche and Chimú art.

JAGUARS AND OTHER CREATURES

The religious imagery of Andean and Pacific coastal cultures was influenced from the earliest times by rainforest animals – jaguars, serpents and other reptiles, monkeys and birds. Aquatic animals, both oceanic and fresh water, and birds were also widespread outside their natural habitats. Such common imagery undoubtedly reflects a basic animism and naturalism in Andean belief. It is also reasoned that the widespread occurrence and repetition of themes infers an underlying universality in the beliefs of Andean cultures.

In particular, both highland and lowland civilizations shared a fascination with the jaguar. The jaguar face inspired the imagery

Right: A sky deity is shown on this Paracas textile with the Oculate Being, complete with serpent tongue, feline whiskers, slithering snakes and streaming trophy heads.

Right: Spiders feature frequently in Andean art, from tiny golden figures on Moche jewellery to this giant Nazca desert geoglyph.

of fanged deities from the earliest times to the Inca Empire. Jaguars were depicted frequently on stationary and portable artefacts –wall paintings, stone carvings, ceramics, textiles and metalwork. Before the prominence of Chavín de Huántar, numerous U-shaped ceremonial centres in the coastal valleys of Peru show an apparently widespread religious coherence, with carvings and paintings of fanged beings at Cardál, Garagay, Sechín Alto, Cerro Sechín, Cabello Muerto, Moxeke and other sites. The plan of Cuzco itself was a feline profile (the shape of a crouching puma), and even the rock at Qenqo, a 'natural' object, was regarded as the profile of a seated puma.

COMPOSITE BEINGS

Composite creatures, combining the features and characteristics of several animals, and human-like beings were also common. Feline-human hybrids, the staff deities (with composite feline face and human body), winged beings, and falcon-headed or other bird-headed warriors all symbolized divinity and were painted and sculpted on ceremonial architecture. The variety of fanged beings implies a wealth of imagination in conjuring up fearful deities to strike awe in the intended worshippers.

In addition, creatures were often shown in cultures that were alien to them. For example, the Tello Obelisk

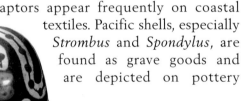

Right: On this Nazca effigy vessel a bird shape is combined with a human face, feline masks and an Oculate Being-like face on the breast.

at Chavín de Huántar shows the creation myth and features the cayman (a jungle creature) in a sierra culture. Mountain raptors appear frequently on coastal textiles. Pacific shells, especially *Strombus* and *Spondylus*, are found as grave goods and are depicted on pottery and architecture throughout the Andean Area. Finally, the ritual pathways of the Nazca trace the outlines of creatures that were alien to the desert, for example a monkey and a whale. Their sacredness was incorporated in the act of following the ritual route. Such representations of 'misplaced' creatures show links between highland and lowland cultures and demonstrate universal reverence.

The Staff Deity of Chavín became a persistent symbol for 1,500 years, with full-frontal beings in various forms featuring widely in Andean art. Its portrayal on the Raimondi Stela epitomizes the Chavín Cult. The full-frontal, standing figure is a composite of animal and human characteristics. Symbols of the Staff Deity, ubiquitous in Chavín imagery, were spread throughout the central and northern Andes and coast on portable art.

Serpents, like felines, were also pan-Andean and were used often in all media: wall paintings, stone carvings, ceramic decoration, textiles and metalwork.

CHAPTER TWO

HONOURING THE GODS

In his *Historia del Nuevo Mundo*, the 17th-century Spanish chronicler and historian Father Bernabe Cobo names 317 different shrines in Inca Cuzco alone. From this, there is no doubt that religion permeated Inca society.

From the earliest times, it is evident that ancient Andean cultures honoured their gods. The treatment shown in special burials and in the construction of special architecture in the midst of domestic dwellings in towns and cities reveals a deep reverence for things beyond day-to-day survival. Whatever their nature, religious considerations were intermixed.

Political arrangements came and went. Rulers were seen to participate in religious ritual, and to be representatives of the gods on Earth. Yet when kingdoms fell and regions were broken up into smaller political entities, the gods remained. In this sense, religion was both integral to and independent of politics in ancient Andean civilization.

The gods and goddesses were depicted on all media: ceramics, textiles and metalwork, and on small and monumental stone, clay and wooden sculpture. They were both portrayed directly, as men and women dressed to represent them, and symbolized in architectural complexes. Features of the landscape were held to be imbued with their presence and therefore representative of them.

Left: Supernatural beings, including a figure reminiscent of the Staff Deity, on a Moche dyed and finely woven cotton textile.

RELIGIOUS CONQUEST

It is not certain, especially in the earliest Andean civilizations, if religion was spread through military conquest. The evidence of the distribution of the art styles and supernatural imagery of different cultures might be interpreted as having been spread through conquest, and the Moche, Wari, Tiwanaku, Chimú and Inca were certainly warlike states engaged in the acquisition of territory through military conquest. The image of the severed head or trophy head was common from the Initial Period onward in virtually every culture. The close association of rule, Inca conquest and the spread of the state cult in the Late Horizon might have been the culmination of a widespread practice.

RELIGION AND ADMINISTRATION

Archaeologists argue that sunken courts and raised platforms, found in both lowland and highland cultures, represent earthly and heavenly deities and themes as well as reflecting the landscapes of the two regions. The central locations of ceremonial complexes among domestic sprawl, or in other cases the isolation of them among surrounding domestic settlements, shows that architectural ceremonial complexes were places for the gathering of people for special rituals. The increasing complexity of elements of ceremonial complexes – divisions into rooms, labyrinthine temples, multiple groupings of platforms, and intricate images of supernatural beings – demonstrates the development of a specialized priesthood to hold the truths of belief and to perform the rituals associated with them.

These centres must also have been places for carrying out civil duties. The sacredness of vital elements – sunshine, water, the well-being of the crops and herds – may have been under the control of the gods, and soliciting the gods' favour may have been the responsibility of the shamans on the peoples' behalf. However, once the crops had been gathered it was the responsibility of a civil structure that had had no direct physical input into their production to administer their distribution.

Thus, the distinction between religion and politics can never have been very clear-cut in ancient Andean cultures.

THE ROLE OF CERRO SECHÍN

The ceremonial complex at Cerro Sechín was built, used and modified over a period of several hundred years. It eventually covered 5ha (12 acres) and must have served as a political and religious centre for a considerable region. Its principal pyramidal structure formed a quadrangle with rounded corners, 53m (174ft) on a side, and its outer wall was adorned with some 400 stone sculptures. The sculptures of the late platform portray humans marching towards a central entrance. They are clearly warriors, and among them are dismembered bodies, severed heads and naked captives. One warrior has severed heads hanging from his waist as trophies.

Below: The cult of Inti was spread throughout the empire through the establishment of Inti-huatana (Hitching Post of the Sun) temples.

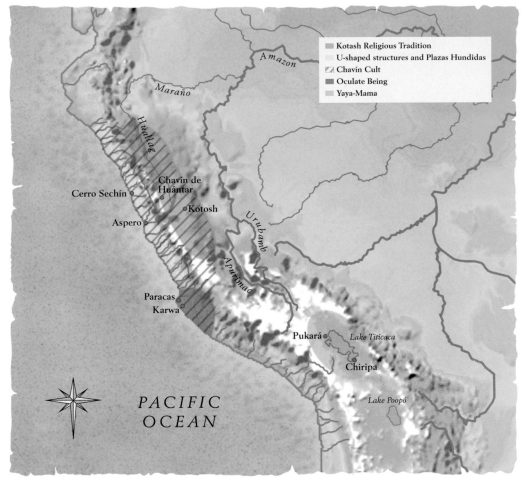

Left: Map showing early religious cults and traditions, including the Kotosh Religious Tradition, the Chavín Cult and Yaya-Mama.

Kotash Religious Tradition
U-shaped structures and Plazas Hundidas
Chavín Cult
Oculate Being
Yaya-Mama

A CONQUERING CULT?

Legends recorded by Spanish chroniclers describe how northern coastal dynasties had been established through invasions from the south. They may be the hazy records of the establishment of the dynasty of Moche lords. Among the Moche, narrative scene painting on pottery and textiles depicts ritual combat and ceremony, including ritual sacrifice. Blood offerings are made to deities impersonated by men and women, presumably priests and priestesses. Burials have been found with elite corpses wearing the costumes depicted in the scenes. This sequence and the scenes might represent the spread of religious ideas with territorial conquest.

The scene seems to show the successful return of an army and can be interpreted as endemic of regional warfare. Yet, this scene is of a late renovation of the Cerro Sechín complex. Was it a war memorial? A stone pilaster of much earlier date depicts essentially the same scene. Or does such repetition over time represent a mythical or legendary battle and victory rather than a specific event? Is it, rather, symbolic of religious conversion combined with territorial claims?

A PEACEFUL CULT?

Archaeologically, the distribution of the symbolic imagery of the Chavín Cult demonstrates it was spread across a large region and that the gods of Chavín were revered among both highland and coastal peoples. Architecturally, Chavín de Huántar was both the inheritor of and participating member in the elements of the ceremonial complex that had developed through the Initial Period and Early Horizon. Yet much of the spread of Chavín religious imagery, especially through portable art, appears to have been achieved alongside the spread of technological innovation.

Like all religious missionaries, those spreading the Chavín Cult would have been faced with explaining complex concepts and evoking other-worldly experiences through objects and representations of them based ultimately on analogy and metaphor.

Chavín artists, either instructed by or acting as shamans, made these themes central to their art. The complexity of Chavín imagery conveys 'otherness'. New techniques in textiles and metallurgy seem to appear suddenly and spread rapidly, conveying the Chavín Cult. This appears to be not military conquest, but rather the perpetuation of regional links already established for economic reasons.

Right: An elaborately decorated Inca wooden kero or drinking vessel in the shape of a head, decorated with figures carrying keros.

ANIMAL AND SUPERNATURAL SYMBOLISM

The fantastic imagery on ancient Andean pottery, textiles, metalwork and stone sculpture is clearly highly symbolic, and it conveyed important meaning to those who knew how to interpret it. Its complexity increased with time to the point where specialized individuals were needed to act as intermediaries between the deities and powers the symbolism represented on the one hand and the general populace on the other.

SHAMANS AND NARRATIVES

The feline and serpentine features that adorned the faces of supernatural beings and humans representing, or being transformed into, them constitute perhaps the most notable imagery used through time and throughout the civilizations of the Andean Area. Close seconds are the uses of birds of all kinds, and of spiders and crabs, particularly in coastal cultures, and the use of double-headed imagery. The general image of the Chavín Staff Deity, by repetition over a widespread area and through time, is a familiar symbol of sacredness and representative of a god and goddess.

More generally, there are several themes that can be identified. Shamanic expression is one that seems easy to recognize. The staring eyes, deep incisions and transfixed expressions on many painted, woven and sculptured faces depict shamans in the state of trance experiencing visions under the influence of hallucinogenic drugs. The contexts of their portrayal, for example a shamman administering to a 'patient' or in a state of transformation into an animal or into a supernatural being, makes this clear.

Another theme is the narrative. Many scenes show a ritual in the process of being performed. This is the case on much Nazca and Moche pottery, on which sacrifices and ritual combat are depicted. Series of images, such as those of shamans and jaguars on the walls

at Chavín de Huántar, give a still-photo-like sequence of transformation. Other scenes imply movement and a 'story', as they depict a hunting or a fishing scene. A sense of perspective is given by overlapping limbs and other elements. Some other scenes show what appear to be obvious themes, such as hunting or fishing, or the harvest on Nazca pots, or battle scenes on Moche and Wari pottery, but these pictures can also carry more complex, extended or additional meanings.

Above: Detail on an early Nazca burial shroud of the sun god, symbolically shown in human form with main and fine rays.

ADDITIONAL MEANINGS

The Nazca 'harvest festival' textile, at face value, shows the produce of the harvest. In detail, however, the Staff Deity-like stance of the figures, their masked or supernatural faces, their complex interlocking pattern and the fact that some are upright and others upside down all contribute to an appearance of hidden or

Right: Regional deities incorporated symbolic themes, as in this Paracas embroidered burial mantle depicting a feline with eyes reminiscent of the staring Oculate Being.

less obvious meanings connected with the ritual significance of the harvest in Nazca religious belief.

Similarly, in the Moche mural (now destroyed) called *The Revolt of the Objects*, everyday objects employ weapons to attack humans. For every human depiction, there is a reciprocal object, such as a warrior with a fox head or a boat with legs, representing duality.

MYSTERIOUS SYMBOLISM

The Moche culture had waned by about the end of the 8th century AD, yet in the 16th century a story about the revolt of 'inanimate' things was told to the Spaniards, seemingly as a general folk story or myth. The survival of the legend for nearly a millennium reveals its apparent common acceptance.

Knowledge that the Inca (and presumably pre-Inca cultures) viewed their world differently from Europeans by regarding virtually everything, including the actual

landscape, as living parts in the universe gives a symbolic meaning to a story that Westerners find difficult to interpret. Other themes are equally complex and difficult to interpret, if they can be interpreted now at all. The symbolism of the Lanzón monolith at Chavín is easier to identify than to interpret. There are two caymans. But why is a river creature featured as the primary deity in a sierra culture? And why, in a culture that existed more than a millennium and a half before the Incas, with their belief in the upper and lower world spheres, are the caymans pointing in celestial and earthly directions?

Left: Detail of three supernatural beings on a Moche cotton textile, one with a staff and, perhaps, a representation of the cratered moon, Si, the northern coastal moon goddess.

SYMBOLIC MEANING

The complexity of Andean Area religion and its different worldview have led scholars to conclude that ancient Andeans infused all their art with potential double meaning. There are images that are real, others that are unreal, and yet others that are purely symbolic. Even real images may operate on a higher symbolic level as well as simply depicting, for example, a man leading a llama or a woman weaving. Does a Moche scene of a man hunting simply portray the act of hunting, or are we meant to be reminded of male characteristics, man's role in society or, perhaps, of a symbolic hunt? Does a female figurine represent a woman, or should it indicate fertility, or, higher still, the mother of humans?

The frequent repetition of such 'scenes' indicates that they are not to be taken at face value. It seems that on one level the essence of appearance is operative and on another level that a hidden, double or reciprocal meaning is operating.

Below: Agricultural abundance is symbolized in this Nazca bridge-spouted vessel, showing a man grasping a maize plant with bulbous roots and laden with ripening cobs.

Many Moche faces painted on pottery, as ceramic effigies or in precious metal, show what appear to be laughing faces but could be snarling or shamanic hysteria.

Some ritual practices are plainly depicted on pots, especially on Moche fine-line red-on-white narrative scenes. Some show blood sacrifices and offerings to deities, or to humans representing deities. Others show individuals engaged in combat. However a closer examination is necessary to see that the combat scenes, for example, show Moche fighting Moche, not a war against Moche enemies. A Nazca stepped-bridged double-spouted vessel painted with a battle scene of interlocking warriors in brilliantly coloured regalia appears equally straightforward. But is this a war of conquest or a depiction of a mythical battle, a symbolic representation of some universal religious 'event' to remind viewers of how the world began and how it operates?

COMPOSITE IMAGERY

Humans with animal heads and other features, a conflated man and peanut or an owl with a trumpet are clearly unreal but may be deeply symbolic of something that we cannot now fully understand. Male and female effigies are clearly shamans by their contexts and visages, but we are unable to understand the full symbolism of the imagery within its own cultural context. The conclusion that the scenes on Moche pots were mythologically symbolic of general religious belief, however, is strengthened by the elite burials of individuals dressed in the identical regalia shown in the narrative scenes.

SYMBOLIC ORGANIZATION

The manner of the organized production of ceramics is itself symbolic. In the Moche and later states, if not earlier, specialists were employed to make thousands of highly crafted pieces as a state-supported enterprise. Many are from burials and seem to have been produced

Above: The meaning of this Moche prisoner effigy vessel is unmistakable: bound wrists and a rope around his head and penis show capitulation, defeat and domination.

specifically for the burial rite. Such a set-up was representative of the power of the state – to command and control ceramic manufacture – and of social organization – part of the populace producing essentials and sharing them with another part through state redistribution of wealth. They are symbolic of the ancient Andean belief that such an arrangement was necessary because not having it would neglect religious belief. Similar arrangements prevailed for the manufacture of precious metal objects, textiles, featherwork and other materials.

For example, there were ceramic work-shops at the Moche towns of Galindo and Cerro Mayal. The Cerro Mayal workshop occupied 29,000 sq ft (9,000 sq m). These towns were the western equivalent, perhaps, of a town with a car factory, wherein much of the local economy was focused on the factory employment.

LOCAL HEROES

The sacrificial scenes on Moche red-on-white painted narratives show not just ordinary citizens, but also combatants who were elites. If not actually of the ruling class, they were at least specialists in their role in ritual combat. Just as potters were state specialists, they also were chosen and trained into the role that they are shown performing. Recent research on Moche effigy pots by Christopher Donnan has produced convincing arguments that the Moche, seemingly unique among pre-Hispanic Andean cultures, actually produced portraiture. More than 900

Below: Detail of a Nazca embroidered textile showing a priest in a tunic displaying the ray-headed Staff Deity, and himself in a similar pose, holding a staff and a trophy head.

Above: Drawings of the Revolt of the Objects, *an Andean mythological theme that survived to Inca times. The original was at the Moche Huaca de la Luna.*

examples are known to show individuals with such distinctive facial features that they cannot be anything other than true likenesses. If they had other meaning as well, this may have been in combination with the use to which they were put, rather than what they depicted.

Their symbolism is revealed by the fact that they were not just one-off portraits, but that groups of them were portraits of the same individual as he grew up. One group, for example, portrays just such an individual who was chosen, trained for ritual combat, was successful in his youth, but was eventually defeated and submitted to sacrifice. His body was dismembered and his blood offered to the gods. The entire sequence of his life, including the manufacture of the effigy vessels to record it, represents a sort of legend and symbolic example. This is symbolism on the order of commemorative event ceramics, coronation crockery, and modern celebrity memorabilia.

REPETITIVE ADDITIONS

Such symbolism and theme-related 'decoration' continued to be the practice in later periods, with certain modifications. Much Wari decoration is geometric and

reflects systematic divisions of space similar to their architecture. Late Intermediate Period art shows a tendency to be additive and non-individualistic, to represent an assembly of elements in repetitive patterns. Yet, among the repetition there is often an anomaly – a singular shape and/or colour that contrasts with the rest of the pattern. Does this represent individual expression in an otherwise rigid society? Or perhaps some understood, and necessary, break in perfection?

Royal and elite cult practice became even stronger, particularly in the Chimú state, in which a huge area of the capital was devoted to enclosed compounds as the palaces of deceased royals, their relations, and their living entourages and dedicated caretaker priests. The entire arrangement was state supported, like the manufacture of pottery and other artefacts, as part of the cult. Once again, the organization symbolized and reinforced the rigid social framework, state power and territorialism.

RITUAL SYMBOLISM IN ARCHITECTURE

Ancient Andean architecture, like portable artefacts, incorporated multiple meanings. From the earliest ceremonial complexes of the Initial Period, once special architecture became the focus of settlement ritual, the architecture and its decoration symbolized religious belief.

CLASSIFICATIONS OF SPACES

Ritual space comprised positive volume, negative volume and neutral areas. Platforms and stepped pyramids were positive structures that mimicked the surrounding landscape of hills and mountains. Negative spaces – sunken courtyards, temple interiors and walled compounds – mimicked natural voids such as caves, valleys and gullies. Walled compounds divided space into territories to confine people, things and activities within the compound, and to restrict some people from the space. Neutral space can be conceived in the more open areas of ceremonial complexes, such as larger courts at ground level, or particularly large walled areas, in which the general public could be accommodated to witness and participate in part in ritual ceremonies.

Above: The double-headed rainbow deity in sculpted mud plaster decorates the platform walls at Huaca el Dragón, near Chan Chan.

Below: Stone heads at Tiwanaku perpetuated a long tradition of decapitation and trophy-head cults, also prominent in the Chavín Cult.

Within neutral space the public could be included as far as they were allowed by the specialists. Their activities could thus be controlled by the ruling elite and specialist religious leaders.

Architectural spaces thus represented specialized areas where ritual enactment could proceed in a controlled manner. The spaces themselves symbolized part of the ritual.

COLOURS AND SOUNDS

Decoration on architecture also symbolized religious concepts. The bright colours painted on sculptural adornment were signals, although their meanings are only generally understood by reference to Inca records from the Spanish chroniclers. The effort to produce the pigments and the use of such bright and numerous shades indicates an early significance, even if their exact meanings are unknown. Apart from anything else, the colours drew attention to the sculpture and architecture, enforcing the presence of the deities portrayed and invoking awe within the beholder. For example, the gaze of the fearsome-looking supernatural face

Above: Even minor detail was symbolic. Here two shaped white stones represent the sacred condor's bill at a fountain at Machu Picchu.

of the Decapitator God on the platform walls and Great Plaza of the Huaca de la Luna at Moche cannot be escaped.

Similarly, there is some evidence for the use of sound. Various shell and pottery trumpets, and drums, must have been used in ritual, and their full effect would have been best appreciated from the heights of platforms by a congregation below. The ritual use of water, channelled through temples and compounds, is notable at Chavín de Huánta (where it is linked to sound), at Tiwanaku and in Cuzco, showing that the practice was a long tradition from the Early to the Late Horizon. It can only reflect the importance of water in ancient Andean survival and agriculture, as benign and life-giving rains filled the lakes and rivers, but also as the power of the weather gods and the forces of storms and thunder. It has been argued that the intricate channelling of water within the temple interiors at Chavín de Huántar was deliberately used to replicate the roar of the elements, from the temple to a presumably awestruck congregation in the courtyard outside.

PATHWAYS AND PROCESSIONS

The ritual pathways of the Nazca lines and of the Inca *ceque* lines represent architectural extensions. 'Owned' by selective groups, they represented symbolic procedures and procession routes. As well as geometric designs similar to those used on pottery and textiles, the Nazca lines and other geoglyphs form the shapes of animals and plants that were held sacred. Such animals were recognized as representative of religious concepts and powers. Large cleared rectangular areas among the Nazca geoglyphs presumably also served as arenas for group ceremonies.

The *ceque* routes of the Incas were both physical and theoretical. They were actual roads followed by intended victims, leading up to their ritual sacrifice, and also lines of sight for astronomical observation and priestly divination. *Ceque* lines divided up the space between them into sacred parcels. Along them, architectural elements were encountered (natural rock outcrops, sometimes modified, caves and springs) and man-made temples.

Moche murals display ritual processions, again in bright colours. They hark back to the single-colour procession of warriors around the platform at Cerro Sechín, one of Moche's predecessors in the north coast valleys. These murals, along with similar scenes on ceramics and elite burials with the costumes of the scenes' participants, are known to depict ritual combat, sacrifices and blood-offerings dedicated to powerful and demanding gods and goddesses.

PAN-ANDEAN SYMBOLISM

Such careful organization of space and the use of prescribed ritual routes were incorporated into Andean religious thought from the first ceremonial complexes. They are recognizable in the U-shaped complexes of the northern coastal valleys and sierra; in the Nazca platforms and plazas of Cahuachi; in the carefully laid-out courts and temples of Chavín de Huántar; in the great mound complexes of 'mountains' on the coast built by the Moche; in the temple-topped pyramid and open plazas of Pachacamac; in the multiple platforms and walled courts of Tiwanaku; in the rigidly organized architecture of Wari central sierra cities; in the sacred royal compounds of Chan Chan of the Chimú; and in the ritual layout of puma-shaped Cuzco and the Sacsahuaman angular-walled Temple to the Sun. The repeated use of the same fundamental forms reveals the underlying essence of the most ancient Andean creation beliefs.

Below: A procession of naked slaves or war captives decorates the Moche pyramid-platform of El Brujo.

COLOURS AS SYMBOLS

The use of bright colours to decorate ceramics, textiles, and adobe and stone sculpture in ancient Andean cultures was universal. From the earliest times, ceramics were painted, textiles featured a variety of dyed colours and were painted on, and murals and sculptures were painted. Stone and metal were often chosen for their colours to create contrast and symbolic statements.

Black, white, green, blue, yellow and shades of red were the primary colours used. Although such deliberate use of colour must reflect metaphorical meaning, its specifics cannot be known with certainty.

EARLY COLOURING

The Initial Period adobe sculptures at Moxeke and Huaca de los Reyes/Caballo Muerto, and the Cerro Sechín sculptured stone slabs were all originally painted in reds, blue and white. The use of black limestone and white granite on the Black

Below: Vivid use of red on an Inca wooden kero drinking cup symbolizes domination and perhaps blood in a llama-herding scene.

Above: Black llamas, much rarer than white and grey ones, were especially sacred and valuable for sacrifices as well as their wool.

and White Portal of the New Temple at Chavín de Huántar was a deliberate choice, and must have been meant to convey a statement: juxtaposing two opposites, and reflecting duality and the opposing forces of nature. As well as the choice of stone colours, the two columns were carved with a male hawk and a female eagle, reinforcing the message.

On Chavín textiles, the background colour was laid out first, then design lines filled in with blue, gold and green threads. Nazca potters perfected no fewer than 13 ceramic slip colours, and such deliberate craftsmanship and choice reflects the importance that colours had in the culture.

The juxtaposition of contrasting colours was a universal practice, presumably a visual symbol of duality and opposition. In Wari art the use of one contrasting colour within a general scheme of harmonious colours must have conveyed some meaning to those who knew how to interpret it. Metallurgists' choice of metals frequently contrasted gold and silver, presumably for the same purpose.

BLUE

Spanish chroniclers recorded some colour meanings among the Inca. How far this can be projected into pre-Inca times is unknown.

The *Huarochirí Manuscript* describes Huatya Curi, son of the sky god Paria Caca. In one of his many contests with his hostile brother-in-law, he danced in a blue feather tunic and white cotton breechcloths, the colours of the sky and clouds, worn, presumably, to honour his father. The Inca rarely used blue, but this colour became more common in clothing in colonial times.

RED

This colour was favoured in Moche ceramics and textiles. Red-on-white fine-line narrative drawings were a Moche speciality. Many narrative scenes show ritual sacrifice, and it is assumed that red is therefore symbolic of blood. It might also be representative of the dawn and dusk skies, when sacrifices might have been performed, also of mud-laden rivers during the rainy season in north coast valleys.

The Incas associated red with conquest and rulership, as blood and perhaps symbolizing conspicuousness. The Inca state insignia, Mascaypacha, comprised a crimson tassel hung from a braid tied around the head. The chronicler Murúa says that each woollen red thread represented a conquered people and the blood of an enemy's severed head. Red seems to have become symbolic of the long tradition of severed heads that began as early as the stone panels at Initial Period Cerro Sechín.

The Inca founder Manco Capac wore a bright red tunic when he stood on the hill of Huanacauri to impress the populace. His 15th-century successor Pachacuti wore a long red robe when he confronted the giant storm god who came down the River Urubamba wreaking destruction.

Inca ritual face-painting featured a red stripe from ear to ear across the bridge of the nose. Sometimes pigment was used,

Below: This Moche scene shows a sacred sky serpent across the stirrup spout and a fishing boat representing the abundance of the sea.

but at other times the blood of a sacrificed llama or the blood of a child *capacocha* sacrifice was used. The blood was smeared across the face of the deceased Inca's mummy to emphasize and enforce the bond of conquered peoples to the living emperor.

Coloured threads and combinations of threads in *quipu* recording devices were also used to represent commodities and perhaps directions, places and numbers.

GREEN

In contrast to red, the Incas associated green with tropical peoples and lands. When Inca Roca, sixth emperor, marched against the rainforest Chunchos of Antisuyu, he went in the guise of a jaguar, donned a green mantle and adopted tropical habits such as chewing coca and tobacco, both green.

The significance of the green stone idol, Yampallec, brought by the legendary conqueror and dynasty founder Naymlap to the north coast, is unknown. The dynasty must have associated green stone with ritual and rule.

Green was also associated with the rainy season, a somewhat obvious link with plant growth and, by extension, with sorcery, drugs and love. Finally, the chronicler Betanzos describes the association of green with ancestors: Pachacuti Inca's kin group washed and dyed themselves with a green herbal plant.

BLACK

Black was fundamentally a metaphor for creation and origins. The Incas, and presumably pre-Inca cultures, associated black with death. In the Camay Quilla ceremony (January/ February) to officially end the rainy season, celebrants dressed in black clothing and blackened their faces with soot. They held a long rope wrapped around the emperor, and newly initiated teenage boys held a mock battle in black tunics. A year after the death of an emperor, his kin group

Above: An Inca noble painted on a wooden kero *drinking cup is dressed in symbolic red, representing conquest and rulership.*

painted their faces black and held a ceremony with his mummified body. Four men with blackened faces concluded the ceremony at the time that it was believed the spirit of the dead Inca arrived at its destination.

Black llamas were sacrificed in the same month, to signify reciprocal ties between the Inca ruler and his subjects. Men dressed in black performed the Mayucati ritual – throwing the ashes of the year's sacrifices into the River Ollantaytambo and following it out of Cuzco by night. The ashes were carried though conquered lands and ultimately to sea as offerings to Viracocha, the supreme deity.

The black-cloud constellations of Inca cosmology, comprising the spaces between stars, were believed to be sources of life and fecundity. They were linked to the colours of the rainbow by association with the deep purple stripe, which the Incas considered the first colour, representing Mama. The remaining colours, called 'lower thing' and 'next thing' descending in colour intensity, were held to descend from Mama.

PILGRIMAGE AND ORACLE SITES

The difficulties inherent in explaining supernatural concepts through images difficult to produce with the existing technology may have fostered the growth of pilgrimage centres. Their symbolic art, meant to show the complexities of supernatural belief, could be combined with complex architecture and mystery in a central place. The spread of religious ideas could be accomplished by bringing converts to a place held most sacred and then dispersing them again, convinced of or reinforced in their belief in the cult. Portable art decorated with the symbolic images of the religious concepts would help remind those living at distance from the cult centre of the tenets of the cult.

Similarly, the sacredness of a cult centre, where the truth was held and expounded by its priests, would become a focus for other-worldly experience. The architecture of the centre could provoke and enhance such an experience.

Below: The Semi-subterranean Court enclosed formal ritual space at Tiwanaku, capital city of the Titicaca Basin.

A WESTERN VIEW?

These general concepts seem self-evident, yet they are overlain with concepts of conversion and missionary work as documented in Western European and North American historical experience. This experience may be different from, and so not directly applicable to, ancient Andean religious experience, for which there is essentially no archaeological evidence.

The growth in the importance of special sites as religious cult centres is not unique to Andean civilization. It is, however, a centrally important part

Above: The city of Pachacamac endured as a powerful centre of religious devotion to the supreme being for more than a millennium.

of ancient Andean belief from at least the Early Horizon. The central location of ceremonial complexes either within a domestic settlement or among surrounding domestic settlements began in the preceding Initial Period. Many sites are identified by scholars as pilgrimage sites: Chavín de Huántar, Cahuachi, Pukará, Tiwanaku, Pachacamac and Inca Cuzco itself.

THE PACHACAMAC MODEL

It is the Spanish colonial records describing the cult and oracle at Pachacamac that provide the basis for the model of ancient Andean pilgrimage and oracle sites. Essential elements of the Pachacamac model were a special chamber housing a cult idol, access to which was restricted to specialist priests; oracular predictions; public plazas for general ritual; and the establishment of a network of affiliated shrines in other communities.

CHAVÍN DE HUÁNTAR

The earliest widely recognized cult centre in ancient Andean civilization was Chavín de Huántar, for it appears to fulfil at least some of these criteria. Its complex architecture deliberately instilled a sense of mystery, supernatural presence and exclusiveness. First the Old Temple, then

the much larger New Temple, comprised numerous interconnected chambers holding a cult monolith carved with the symbolic image of a supernatural being. Its isolation within the temple clearly restricted access to it and made it more awesome and powerful. Its complex symbolic imagery made it necessary for specialists to interpret it.

The Old Temple contained the Lanzón, or Great Image, monolith and the New Temple held the Raimondi Stela. The curious position of the former, piercing through the roof of one chamber to a hidden upper chamber, implies an oracular room. The acoustics of the water channels of the temples also implies the mysterious use of echoing and mimicry of the elements.

Both the Old Temple and the New Temple were accompanied by open plazas. These were wide, flat spaces between the arms of the U-shaped platform mounds, and within each was a sunken ceremonial courtyard: round in the Old Temple, square in the New Temple.

The imagery of several Chavín deities became widespread: the Staff Deity and feline and serpent imagery in particular. Yet, felines and serpents were common elements in earlier cultures throughout an even wider area. Several sites, however, show imagery, though locally produced, that is identical to that from Chavín.

At Huaricoto, north-west of Chavín, the Early Horizon ritual precinct contained a carved stone 'spatula' depicting the deity of the Lanzón. There is also decorated pottery of Chavín design. Other sites in adjacent highlands also have portable artefacts of Chavín style. It may be, however, that the Chavín Cult was adopted in addition to established local patron deities.

More revealing is Karwa on the southern coast, near the Paracas necropolis site. Textiles from the Karwa tomb are

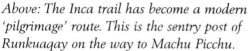

Above: The Inca trail has become a modern 'pilgrimage' route. This is the sentry post of Runkuaqay on the way to Machu Picchu.

decorated not in the local Paracas style but in the bright colours and images of the Chavín Cult, including their composition, bilateral symmetry and double profiling. The Chavín Staff Deity, here in female form and sometimes called the Karwa Goddess, is unmistakable. Such faithful adherence to the Chavín orthodoxy seems to betray Chavín presence or a shrine in a network of Chavín shrines.

In the northern highlands, Chavín stone sculpture from Kuntur Wasi and Pacopampa clearly displays Chavín imagery. In the upper Lambayeque river drainage, two matching carved stone columns were found, reminiscent of the Black and White Portal columns at Chavín de Huántar. Further, in the Chicama Valley there were painted adobe columns (now destroyed), one of which was painted with a winged creature like those on the Black and White Portal.

The distribution of these sites across cultural spheres and production zones indicates the establishment of Chavín shrines and may imply the integration of the cult into local community structures.

Left: Chavín de Huántar became the earliest widely recognized pilgrimage and oracular site in the Early Horizon.

TEMPLES AND SUNKEN COURTS

The earliest ceremonial complexes in the northern coastal valleys and adjacent northern Peruvian sierra organized both positive and negative space in the forms of platforms and sunken courts. The forming of a U-shape, comprising a tiered platform at the base and two elongated platform wings enclosing a sunken court and a level, open plaza around it, was clearly symbolic. The form was repeated at numerous coastal valley and northern and central Peruvian highland sites. Its mere repetition underlies a core of common religious belief.

U-SHAPE ORIGINS

The U-shaped ceremonial structure was the culmination of the development of two elements: platforms and subterranean courts. The U-shaped temple established at Chavín de Huántar as the centre of a religious cult had representations as far afield as the southern coastal valleys. But the form began much earlier, in the Initial Period.

The building of platform mounds began at least as early as 3000BC. The earliest were those at Aspero in the Supe Valley: the Huaca de los Idolos and the Huaca de los Sacrificios, among a ceremonial complex of as many as 17 platforms. Within the next few centuries

Below: The mud-plaster walls of the Middle Temple at Garagay feature a fanged being with spider attributes and water symbolism.

smaller complexes of mounds had been built at Piedra Parada, also in the Supe Valley, El Paraíso in the Chillón Valley, Río Seco in the Chancay Valley, Bandurria in the Huaura Valley, Salinas de Chao and Los Morteros in the Chao Valley, and at Kotosh, a highland site in the Río Huallaga-Higueras Valley.

Ancient Andeans were thus building ceremonial architecture as early as the first royal pyramids in Egypt and temple platforms, called ziggurats, in ancient Mesopotamia; and Andean ceremonial platforms are the earliest in the New World, predating the first Olmec earthen pyramids in Mesoamerica by at least 1,000 years.

Two 'traditions' of raised platforms developed, both based on ritual on top of the platform and open ceremonial space at the base for an attendant congregation: the Supe-Aspero Tradition and the El Paraíso Tradition. Chambers and niches to house ritual objects were built on top as the traditions evolved.

The practice of building circular sunken courts (*plazas hundidas*) also began in northern Peru during the 2nd millennium BC. Most often they were built in association with a platform at its base and aligned with the platform's staircase. Early examples include Salinas de Chao, Piedra Parada and highland La Galgada.

Above: The great temple pyramid platform of Huaca Larga incorporated La Ray Mountain in the centre of the Moche city Tucume Viejo.

Only occasionally was a sunken court built as the sole ceremonial element, for example at Alto Salavery.

By about 2000BC the stone-built civic-ceremonial centre at El Paraíso was the largest Preceramic Period civic-ceremonial centre on the coast. With a group of small temples forming a base and two elongated parallel platforms, it was a configuration transitional to the classic U-shaped structures of the Initial Period.

Below: Huaca de la Luna, mimicking the hill behind it, another Moche mud-brick temple of the Early Intermediate Period.

SECHÍN ALTO

By 1200BC the U-shaped ceremonial complex at Sechín Alto was the largest civic-ceremonial complex in the New World. At its fullest development it included all the elements of the classic U-shaped ritual centre. Construction began in about 1400BC (although one radiocarbon date from the site is as early as 1721BC). Its principal platform ruin still stands some 44m (144ft) above the plain and covers an area 300 x 250m (985 x 820ft). The huge U-shape is formed by sets of parallel platform mounds extending from the base corners of the pyramid, and forming part of a ritual area 400 x 1,400m (1,310 x 4,600ft). Running north-east from the principal pyramid is a succession of plazas and sunken courts.

The principal wings enclose a plaza with an early, small sunken court. Beyond the ends of these mounds there is a larger circular sunken court, then another open area formed by two long, thin parallel platforms flanking a plaza approximately 375m (1,230ft) square. Forming the end of the complex, 1km (½ mile) north-east of the principal platform, an H-shaped platform faces the main pyramid and flanks the largest circular sunken court, 80m (262ft) in diameter. The principal pyramidal platform is faced with enormous granite blocks set in clay mortar. Some of the blocks are up to 1.4m (4.5ft) on each side and weigh up to 2 tonnes (tons).

Surrounding the Sechín Alto complex there was 10.5 sq km (2,560 acres) of buildings and smaller platforms.

Above: The high stone walls of the rectangular Semi-subterranean Court at Tiwanaku were decorated with stone trophy heads.

Like other U-shaped complexes, the site must have been a religious centre that served its surrounding area. Judging by its size, it may have served a considerable region as well.

RITUAL MEANINGS

The practical aspects of the arrangements of the U-shaped complex seem obvious: a raised platform from which to address a crowd, an open area for the crowd to stand in and a sunken court for exclusive ritual. There is an element of implied control in the arrangement: the congregation was partly confined between the arms of the U-shape, and their attention could be monitored from the height of the platform or focused on the sunken court.

Perhaps the two elements symbolize the concepts of a sky deity and an earth deity. Ritual may have involved procession from one to the other. Assuming strong naturalism in early Andean religious thought, the gods were believed to inhabit or infuse the natural landscape. Thus platforms were representative mountains and sunken courtyards representative valleys or caves. Further, their shapes might have represented the sky father and the earth mother, the womb and the symbolic shapes of man and woman. In seeming recognition of the source of life-giving water as the mountain thunder and rainstorms, the open ends of U-shaped complexes were oriented towards the mountains, their U-shapes imitating the collecting valleys.

Below: The ultimate sacred circular court of the great Sacsahuaman Temple of Cuzco formed the puma's head of the Inca capital.

SACRED CEMETERIES

Honouring the gods in the southern coastal desert cultures was focused on cemetery rites and ancestor worship. The dry climate has been instrumental in preserving the buried bodies and artefacts in the tombs.

SHARED TRADITIONS

The Paracas and Nazca cultures developed in continuous succession through the Early Horizon and Early Intermediate Period in the southern valleys and deserts of Peru, focusing their settlement and economy around sea fishing and shellfish collecting, and later on maize and cotton agriculture. Early Paracas ceramics and textile decoration shows much influence from Chavín de Huántar. At Karwa, near the early Paracas necropolis, textiles from an elite tomb are decorated with one of the best representations of the Staff Deity. Here she is the Staff Goddess, thought to honour a local goddess while at the same time acting as a 'wife' or 'sister' shrine to the Chavín Cult in the north.

Below: Stone slab circles at the Sillustani necropolis of the Colla people possibly served as the sites of burial ceremonies before bodies were taken to their kinship chullpa *tower.*

The Paracas and Nazca developed their own distinct style and deities. Quintessential was the Oculate Being, a wide-eyed distinctively local deity depicted in brightly painted ceramic masks and portrayed, flying, on pottery and textiles.

THE CAVERNAS CEMETERY

Paracas settlements covered an area of some 54ha (133 acres) around a core area of about 4ha (10 acres) on the low slopes of the Cerro Colorado on the Paracas Peninsula. Among the sprawling habitation remains, special areas were used as cemeteries for hundreds of burials, possibly the foci of family cults for nearby and more distant settlements.

Great care was taken in the burial of the dead in the Cavernas cemetery area. The naked corpse was tied with a cord into a flexed seated position. The body was wrapped in several layers of richly coloured textiles, both cotton and wool, revealing trade contact with highland cultures for llama wool. Placed in a basket and accompanied by plain and richly decorated ceramics, and sheet-metal jewellery, the whole was finally wrapped in plain cotton cloth. Such 'bundles' were

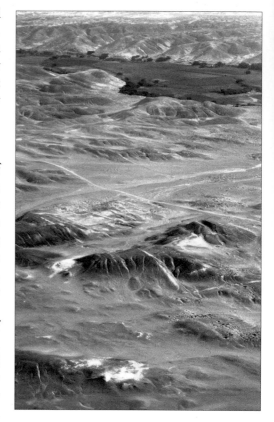

Above: Cahuachi, a sacred 'city' of about 40 temple mounds, served as a funerary and pilgrimage centre for Nazca religion.

then enshrined in large subterranean crypts, which were reopened and used repeatedly over generations, presumably by kin groups as family mausoleums.

PARACAS INFLUENCE

A prominent element in Paracas and Nazca religious ritual was decapitation. Trophy heads adorn pottery and stream from the waists of Oculate Beings on textiles. In addition, the skulls of many Paracas burials show evidence of ritual surgery, with small sections of the cranium being removed by incision and drilling. The exact purpose of this operation is unknown – it may have been ritual or medical. The Nazca inherited veneration of the Oculate Being from the Paracas culture.

Highland drought had caused increasing aridity in the coastal plains. It seems likely, therefore, that the Oculate Being was

associated with water and precipitation. Flying Oculate Beings perhaps betray a fixation with the sky. As a practical measure, the Nazca developed an elaborate system of underground aqueducts to collect and channel the maximum amount of water around Cahuachi. Great stepped spiral galleries, cobbled with smooth river stones, gave access to the wells.

Two of the most important Nazca settlements were Cahuachi and Ventilla, the first a ritual 'city', the second an urban 'capital'. Ventilla covered an area of at least 200ha (495 acres) with terraced housing, walled courts and small mounds. It was linked to Cahuachi by a Nazca line across the intervening desert.

Revealing their wide Andean contacts, Nazca ceramics and textiles are also decorated with a multitude of supernatural, clearly symbolic images. As well as sea creatures, crabs, insects and serpents that would have been familiar local sights, images of monkeys, felines and tropical birds from the rainforests were also used.

Below: In the Nazca cemetery (and Paracas, shown above) of the southern desert coast cultures, the desiccated conditions preserved the hair, fibres and textiles of the deceased.

The trophy-head cult extended to caches of trepanned, severed skulls of sacrificial victims being found among the remains in Nazca cemeteries.

LINES AND CEREMONIAL MOUNDS

Nazca religion is defined by two elements. Cahuachi was a ritual complex concerned with spiritual matters rather than daily life. Covering an area of 150ha (370 acres), it comprised a complex of 40 ceremonial mounds made by shaping natural hillocks into terracing and associated plazas. It was used from about AD100 to 550, and thereafter continued in use as a mortuary ground and place of votive offering. The entire site appears to have been devoted to mortuary practices, probably as family vaults following the Paracas tradition.

The largest mound was 30m (98ft) high, modified into six or seven terraces with adobe-brick retaining walls. Most of the tombs have been looted, but the few unlooted tombs excavated yielded mummified burials accompanied by exquisitely decorated, multicoloured woven burial coats and ceramics. Some contained animal sacrifices and ritual human sacrifices of Nazca men, women and children. Some skulls had excrement inserted into the mouths; some had been perforated and a

Above: The Paracas cemetery (and Nazca, shown below left) of the Early Horizon and Early Intermediate Period served numerous cities as kinship burial mausoleums.

carrying cord inserted; some had blocked eyes, cactus spines pinning the mouth shut, and tongues removed and put in pouches.

The second element was the Nazca lines, the geoglyphs forming geometric patterns, clusters of straight lines and recognizable animal and plant figures. There are some 1,300km (808 miles) of such lines, including 300 figures. A huge 490m-long (1,600ft) arrow, pointing towards the Pacific Ocean, is thought to be a symbol to invoke rains. The lines were undoubtedly associated with the Nazca preoccupation with water and crop fertility, together with worship of mountain deities – the ultimate source of water.

Cahuachi was abandoned as the coastal valleys became more arid. Simultaneously, there was an increase in the number and elaboration of Nazca lines. Regarded as ritual pathways, perhaps like the family vaults dedicated to kin groups, the increase in their use represents desperate efforts to placate the gods who had forsaken them. As Cahuachi was abandoned, people covered the mounds with layers of sand.

CEREMONIAL COMPOUNDS

Platforms and U-shaped complexes continued to form the core elements of ceremonial centres in the northern coastal valleys and highlands through the Early Horizon. In time, Moche platforms of the Early Intermediate Period achieved both the shape and proportions of hills, as if the people were building their own mountains on the coast. The Huaca del Sol and Huaca de la Luna at Moche are the largest adobe-built pyramidal platforms ever constructed in the Americas.

ALTIPLANO TRADITIONS

In the southern highlands of the Titicaca Basin architectural symbolism also mirrored the landscape. Here there developed a tradition comprising a central platform mound with a central, square sunken court at the top surrounded by rectangular temples arranged symmetrically around the court. This 'tradition' of a sacred compound flourished in the late 2nd and 1st millennia BC and is named after its principal example, Chiripa, near the southern end of Lake Titicaca. Compared to the huge mounds built at U-shaped complexes, Altiplano mounds were relatively modest in scale. The final height of the Chiripa mound, reached late in the 1st millennium BC when the site was used by people from Tiwanaku, was a mere 6m (19½ft).

Below: The ciudadelas *of Chimú and Chan Chan comprised courtyards and chambers for ritual and ceremony as 'cities' of the dead.*

THE PUKARÁ TRADITION

In the Early Horizon, religious and political focus shifted north of the lake during the latter half of the 1st millennium BC and became centred at the site of Pukará, northwest of Lake Titicaca. Unlike U-shaped complexes, the Pukará Tradition comprised monumental masonry-clad structures terraced against hillsides. The principal terrace had a monumental staircase and was topped by a rectangular sunken court with one-room buildings around three sides – a style that was reminiscent of Chiripa.

The Pukará Tradition's religious focus was on the Yaya-Mama cult of male and female symbolism, although it also shared the feline and serpentine imagery prevalent throughout contemporary Andean civilization. This emphasis on father sky and mother earth is reflected not only in the carved images of Yaya and Mama monoliths, but also in the combination of platforms and sunken courts in association with ritual architecture.

These developments were not isolated, however. The economy of the Altiplano was largely based on llama pastoralism and the wool was traded with the southern coastal cultures of Paracas and Nazca and farther

Above: The mud walls and rooms at the Tchudi *ciudadela at Chan Chan were sculpted with attention to detail throughout.*

afield. Thus, religious ideas must have been encountered from northern regions through the Chavín Cult and its aftermath.

THE TIWANAKU COMPOUND

Pukará dominated the Titicaca Basin Altiplano for about four centuries. Its inheritor in the later Early Intermediate Period and the Middle Horizon was Tiwanaku, a ceremonial city of proportions and complexity to rival the waning Chavín de Huántar and any northern and southern coastal valley contemporaries of the Moche and Nazca.

Two rival empires eventually dominated the Middle Horizon: the highland peoples of Tiwanaku and Wari. Although they shared religious concepts, they conquered respective areas and reached an uneasy settlement with each other at a highland boundary in the La Raya Pass south of Cuzco.

Ceremonial buildings at Chiripa and Pukará herald those at Tiwanaku. The tradition of the enclosed courtyard was continued and expanded into large

public, walled ceremonial areas and semi-subterranean courts. Platforms remained relatively low and sunken courts stayed rectangular in shape.

From Tiwanaku, Mt Illimani dominates the view and is perhaps replicated in the platform mound of the Akapana pyramid. In nearby Lake Titicaca sit the Island of the Sun and the Island of the Moon, believed to be the birthplaces of the sun and moon. The moat around the Akapana and Kalasasaya structures renders the complex a symbolic island, although it can be argued that in the flat compound the water in a moat would flood the structural footings and drains. Nevertheless, the essence of the symbolic island is there.

AKAPANA AND THE PUMA PRIEST
The Akapana temple comprised a six-stepped mound in the shape of half a stepped diamond, known as the Andean Cross. The top was occupied by either a palace/temple or by a sunken court in the shape of a full-stepped diamond cross.

Above: Wari's southernmost provincial centre, Pikilacta, was laid out as repetitive, adjoining, symmetrical stone-walled compounds.

Excavations revealed that ritual eating and burials took place there, including the primary burial of a man seated and holding a puma effigy incense burner. There was also a cache of sacrificed llama bones, and most of the skeletons found buried on the first terrace and under its

foundations were headless. The upper terraced walls of the platform were decorated with tenoned stone puma heads, and at the base of the western staircase a black basalt image of a seated, puma-headed person (*chachapuma*) holding a severed head in his lap was found. Another *chachapuma* sculpture is a standing figure holding dangling severed heads.

Such symbolism – severed heads, pumas, the western location indicative of the setting sun and night – implies shamanic ritual, puma transformation and death.

On the huge Sun Gate at Tiwanaku, the central figure has often been associated with the sun, owing to his rayed head. The frontal stance and arms holding staffs equally associate the figure with the Staff Deity of Chavín. Another interpretation, however, can be based on the stepped dais on which the figure stands. It is identical to the half-stepped diamond court of the Akapana and could imply association with the *chachapuma*.

Such complex, composite, enigmatic imagery is typical of the tradition of multiple meanings and hidden or obscure meaning in Andean religious symbolism. Specialists are needed to interpret the imagery, perhaps according to the ceremony and occasion.

Left: In its remote mountain location, Machu Picchu was a sacred Inca city and religious retreat at the heart of the empire.

THE PACHACAMAC NETWORK

The religious network of Pachacamac was organized in sympathy with Andean concepts of community, mutual exchange, taxation and kinship.

THE ORACLE SITE

The cult centre was the city of Pachacamac at the mouth of the River Lurín, south of modern Lima. It comprised a complex of adobe platforms and plazas. An isolated chamber at the summit of the principal platform housed an oracle. There were open plazas in which pilgrims could fast and participate in public ceremony. Access to the oracle chamber was strictly limited to cult specialists. Oracular messages were given by these specialists concerning life and the future: predictions about the weather, favourable interventions of the gods with the elements, protection

Below: Pachacamac, established in the 3rd century AD, soon became a cult centre for the supreme deity, Pachacamac.

against diseases, specialized knowledge about the best times for planting and the harvest. Earthquakes, crop failure and other disasters were believed to be the result of antagonizing the god Pachacamac.

Much of what is known of the Pachacamac oracle site is from descriptions from Inca and early Spanish colonial sources. The elements of the central coastal ceremonial city incorporated the full range of Andean religious architecture: platform mounds, sacred compounds and plazas for congregational worship, and exclusive chambers for restrictive ritual performed by specialists.

Distant communities solicited the priests for permission to establish branch shrines to Pachacamac. If deemed to have the ability to support cult activities, a priest from Pachacamac was assigned to the new shrine and the community supplied labour on and produce from assigned lands to support him and the shrine. Part was kept for the shrine and

the rest sent to the Pachacamac oracle site. Such branches were thought of as the wives, children or brothers and sisters of the main cult complex.

THE CULT

Pachacamac – 'earth/time maker' – was the creator deity of the peoples of central coastal Peru and the adjacent Andes. The Pachacamac cult and shrine began to become important in the latter half of the Early Intermediate Period. By the 16th century a network of shrines spanned the range of Andean Area production zones from the coast into the highlands, as well as north and south along the coast.

The cult itself spread from the coast, first north and south, then inland into the highlands, where worship of Pachacamac rivalled the highland creator deity Viracocha. Its spread inland is associated with the inland spread of the Andean Area Quechua language.

In the Middle Horizon and Late Intermediate Period the cult and oracle site overtook the importance of local deities to the north and south coasts – those of the Nazca and Moche. Even when the mountain empire of Wari rose and its armies threatened the coast, ultimately to conquer Pachacamac and incorporate the city into its empire, Pachacamac remained independently important as an oracle site. In fact, despite being politically demoted to an outpost of Wari power, Pachacamac remained religiously important throughout the Late Intermediate Period.

When the Incas arrived in the Late Horizon they immediately recognized the importance of the oracle, not only locally but also throughout the region and beyond. They recognized Pachacamac's importance in relation to Viracocha and sought to accommodate the religious concepts that both gods embodied.

The cult thus endured for more than a millennium. In addition to its primary religious purpose, it became entrenched in

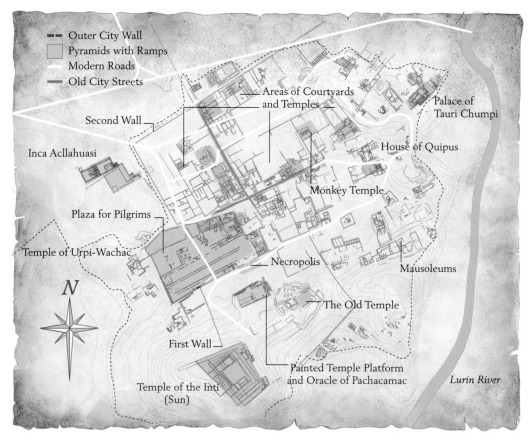

Map legend:
- - - Outer City Wall
- Pyramids with Ramps
- Modern Roads
- Old City Streets

Second Wall
Areas of Courtyards and Temples
Palace of Tauri Chumpi
Inca Acllahuasi
House of Quipus
Monkey Temple
Plaza for Pilgrims
Temple of Urpi-Wachac
Necropolis
Mausoleums
The Old Temple
First Wall
Painted Temple Platform and Oracle of Pachacamac
Lurín River
Temple of the Inti (Sun)
N

the community and its social structure, in its agricultural production and in the redistribution of wealth. There is, however, no recorded evidence of the use of missionaries to spread the cult's ideology.

EARLY ORIGINS

The site of Pachacamac became important locally from the latter half of the Early Intermediate Period, when the first phases of the pyramid platform to the sun and adjoining Temple to Pachacamac were built. It became an important political power during the Middle Horizon, and may have been partly responsible for the northern shift of Moche power in the late Early Intermediate Period/Middle Horizon.

Wari presence is attested by the architecture and a Wari cemetery, and the continuance of the site's religious importance is implied by a wooden post carved with figures of Wari-like divinities, as well as stone figurines. The upper part of the post depicts a man holding a bola and wearing a chest ornament; the lower part is carved with double-headed serpents, jaguars and a figure with attributes like those of the 'angels' on the Gateway to the Sun at Tiwanaku.

LATE HORIZON PACHACAMAC

The 16th-century chronicler Cieza de León noted the importance of the shrine and Inca reverence for it, while the

17th-century writer Father Bernabe Cobo devoted an entire chapter to a detailed description of the ancient site.

Cobo describes how devotees of the Pachacamac Cult visited the centre specifically to petition the priests there to establish satellite shrines in the cities of their homelands, and to permit them to erect 'wife', 'son' or 'daughter' shrines of their local deities, to Pachacamac. Prophecy from the oracle was sought for everything from health, fortune, the well-being of

Below: The Incas recognized Pachacamac's importance, but also built a temple to Inti, the sun god, here.

Above: The main pyramid platform at Pachacamac was surrounded by a vast complex of courtyards and platforms.

crops and flocks, the weather and even the prognosis of Inca battle plans. Defying or neglecting Pachacamac was believed to provoke earthquakes. Offerings in solicitation of oracles included cotton, maize, coca leaves, dried fish, llamas, guinea pigs, fine textiles, ceramic drinking vessels and gold and silver – no doubt useful to the priests.

The arrival of aliens – the Spaniards – caused the oracle to fall silent, although worshippers still visit Pachacamac today to make offerings.

STATE RELIGION

Although the Incas embraced the cults of all those they conquered, and worshipped a pantheon of deities, they insisted on the supremacy of a state religion or cult centred on their own two principal deities: Viracocha and Inti.

Viracocha was more of an all-embracing entity than a specific god or idol. He was not exclusively Inca, rather a long-standing highland creator god. The Inca traced the origin of their right to rule the Andean Area to Viracocha.

Inti, the sun god, was increasingly favoured in day-to-day worship in the late 15th and early 16th centuries, as the empire grew. The importance of the person of the emperor himself was emphasized more, in an attempt to focus the various peoples of the empire on a state cult, not in replacement of long-held beliefs, but to empower the state and enhance the importance of the new regime the Incas brought.

In keeping with Andean pantheism, other major Inca deities were Quilla (moon goddess), Chaska-Qoylor (goddess of Venus), Illapa (weather god: thunder, lightning, rain) and Cuichu (god of the rainbow). The two principal temple complexes in Cuzco were the sacred Coricancha precinct and the imposing Sacsahuaman edifices.

Below: The carved stone walls of the Temple to Inti at the fortress of Ollantatambo – one of many temples spreading the state cult.

Above: This La Tolita (Ecuador) sheet-gold mask of the sun god is similar to the golden image of Inti in the Coricancha Temple.

THE CULT OF INTI

The universality of the sun notwithstanding, the Inca cult of Inti was in many respects unique. The emperor's person became regarded as the earthly embodiment of the sun. His presence and well-being were vital to the life of every subject, and to the prosperity of the land in general. Although the emperor's power was absolute, Inti was believed to be benevolent and generous. Solar eclipses were regarded as signs of his anger and required sacrifice and the solicitation of the return of his favour. As the power of the state cult grew, Inti came to be regarded as Viracocha's intermediary.

By the 16th century Inti/the emperor was so central to the state's well-being that an incident witnessed by priests during ceremonies in his honour appeared to foretell the empire's end. In the reign of Huayna Capac, priests witnessed the fall of an eagle from the sky mobbed by buzzards. The event coincided with reports of the spread of an unknown deadly disease – now known to have been smallpox brought by the Spaniards and spreading from Mesoamerica.

The Coricancha was the centre of the state cult dedicated to Inti's worship. A great mask of sheet gold, moulded into a human face, wide-eyed and grinning, and with rays of zigzag sheet gold ending in miniature masks was housed in its own chamber within the temple.

Rituals and offerings to Inti served constantly to reinforce his power and to confirm the acceptance among the people of the emperor as representing Inti himself. The dead emperor's mummified remains were brought out on ritual occasions, and offered food and drink, and sacrifices, in the belief in the ultimate immortality of Inti.

THE RIGHT TO RULE

Inca right to rule was integral in the state cult. The Incas were painstaking in their efforts to establish, and to alter as necessary, an elaborate mythology to support this close association of Inti, the emperor and power. The Incas demonstrated their right to rule, and unified the empire, by proving that all peoples were descended from the same ancestors, namely the Inca ancestors. The beliefs and cosmologies of those they conquered had to be incorporated into the state religion. To do this alongside continuous acquisition of territories and peoples required an unremitting effort to add to and alter the state mythology. It was important to extend this continuity right back to the first ruler of Cuzco, Manco Capac, and to link the state foundation myth with creation mythology itself.

Official mythology describing the wanderings of the ancestors after their emergence from Tambo Toco cave included the sun's sanction of the founder Manco Capac to rule in his name. In another version Manco Capac is said to have bedecked himself in gold plates to give credulity to his divine appearance when he presented himself at dawn to the people of Cuzco. As the myth was developed, Pachacuti Inca Yupanqui

Below: Machu Picchu was an imperial retreat and sacred city devoted to Inti. This stone-walled chamber was possibly a royal tomb.

Above: The Observatorio at Machu Picchu was the focus of the cult of Inti. Its central window is placed to align with the rising of the sun on the winter solstice (21 June).

(AD 1438–71) added his dream visit and discovery at the spring of Susurpuquio of a crystal tablet bearing the image of Viracocha, who sanctioned his right to rule.

Pachacuti and his son Tupac Inca Yupanqui (1471–93) rebuilt much of Cuzco to accommodate the state cult, including the rebuilding of the Coricancha to enhance the importance of Inti. Thus, the creator, the sun and the emperor were united in one stroke.

ONLY ONE RIVAL

Viracocha's, and therefore Inti's, only serious rival was the cult and oracle of Pachacamac. The site was duly included in the wanderings of Viracocha. The Incas recognized Pachacamac's ancient importance, but to establish the state's supremacy they built a temple to Inti alongside that of the Pachacamac oracle. Pachacamac's importance was noted, but the temple to Inti in the city was more than a reciprocal shrine dedicated to a regional deity.

The peoples of the empire were also continually reminded of their bond with Inti by *capacocha* sacrifices. Annually, chosen victims were brought from the provinces to Cuzco, then marched back out to their respective provinces again for ritual sacrifice in the name of both Inti and the emperor.

THE SACRED CORICANCHA

The Coricancha or Golden Enclosure of imperial Cuzco, was the centre of the Inca cosmos. It was the supreme ceremonial precinct of the capital, the most sacred *huaca*. It housed the images of Viracocha, the creator, and Inti, god of the sun, and other principal Inca deities. From it emanated the sacred *ceque* lines, both physical roads and cosmic routes of sacred meaning. Forty-one *ceques* led to 328 sacred locations: *huacas* such as caves, springs, stone pillars and points on the surrounding horizon, and important locations such as critical junctions of the city's irrigation canals. One Spanish chronicler, Bernabe Cobo, listed 317 shrines.

These lines bound the Inca world, physical and religious, to the Coricancha 'navel' of the world. From points within the precinct, priests plotted the movements

Below: The sacred Coricancha included separate chambers dedicated to and housing the idols of the principal Inca deities.

of Mayu (the Milky Way) across the night sky – for example from the Ushnua Pillar, from which sightings of Mayu were taken between two pillars on the distant horizon.

The complex was in the tail of the puma image profile that formed the plan of Cuzco, at the confluence of the rivers Huantanay and Tullamayo, emphasizing the importance of water in the Andean psyche. The second most sacred shrine of the city, Sacsahuaman, formed the puma's head at the prominence above the rivers.

THE SACRED WASI

The complex is sometimes referred to as the Temple of the Sun (Inti), but in fact, the temple to Inti was one of several temples forming the precinct. It was built of stone blocks so carefully fitted together that there was no need for mortar. Its walls were covered with sheet gold – referred to as 'the sweat of the sun' – while another of the temples, to Quilla, was covered in silver ('tears of the moon').

Above: The entrance to the Golden Enclosure of the Coricancha in Cuzco, centre of the state cult of Inti (the sun god).

The precinct comprised six *wasi*, or covered chambers, arranged around a square courtyard. Each *wasi* was dedicated to one of the six principal Inca state deities: Viracocha, Inti, Quilla, Chaska-Qoylor (Venus as morning and evening star), Illapa (weather, thunder, lightning) and Cuichu (rainbow), ranged hierarchically in that order, although Viracocha and Inti were near equivalents.

Each temple housed an image of the deity and the paraphernalia of ritual and worship. A special room was reserved for the storage and care of the mummies of deceased emperors (*mallquis*). On ritual days – for example the winter and summer solstices of Inti Raymi and Capac Raymi – the *mallquis* were brought out in their rich vestments, carried on royal litters in procession around the capital and offered food and drink while court historians recited their deeds. The temple courtyard was also the venue for incantations to and the sanctification of *capacochas* – specially selected sacrificial victims. From the Coricancha they set out

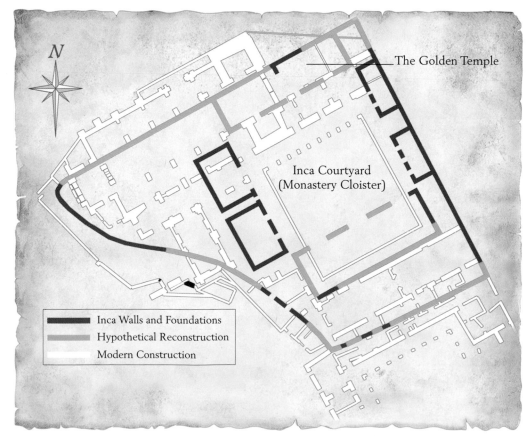

N

The Golden Temple

Inca Courtyard
(Monastery Cloister)

Inca Walls and Foundations
Hypothetical Reconstruction
Modern Construction

Above: Exterior of the Temple of the Moon in the Coricancha, Cuzco, showing the closely fitted blocks without mortar.

on their ritual journey following *ceque* lines back to their provinces, where they were sacrificed.

Other rooms were used to store the sacred objects taken from conquered provinces, including a *huaca* from each subjugated population. These *huacas* were kept in perpetual residence as hostages, and nobles from each subject population were forced to live in the capital for several months each year.

A GOLDEN GARDEN

The intimate mythological connection between Inti and gold was manifested in the temple garden. Here were gold and silver sculptures of a man, a woman, animals and plants representing creation. There were not only jaguars, llamas, guinea pigs and monkeys, but also birds, butterflies and other insects.

The arrangement of the Coricancha was established by the tenth emperor, Pachacuti Inca Yupanqui, in the 15th century, along with his rebuilding of much of the capital.

Something of its splendour was captured in the words of the conquistador Pedro de Cieza de León, as recorded in his *Crónica del Peru*, published in Seville between 1550 and 1553:

'[The temple was] more than 400 paces in circuit…[and the finely hewn masonry was] a dusky or black colour… [with] many openings and doorways… very well carved. Around the wall, half way up, there was a band of gold, two *palmos* wide and four *dedos* in thickness. The doorways and doors were covered with plates of the same metal. Within [there] were four houses, not very large, but with walls of the same kind and covered with plates of gold within and without…. In one of these houses…there was the figure of the Sun, very large and made of gold…enriched with many precious stones.

They also had a garden, the clods of which were made of pieces of gold; and it was artificially sown with golden maize, the stalks, as well as the leaves and cobs, being of that metal … . Besides all this, they had more than 20 golden sheep [llamas] with their lambs, and the shepherds with their slings and crooks to watch them, all made of the same metal. There was [also] a great quantity of jars of gold and silver, set with emeralds; vases, pots, and all sorts of utensils, all of fine gold.'

It was with this golden wealth of the Coricancha that Atahualpa attempted to secure his freedom when he was captured and imprisoned by Francisco Pizarro at Cajamarca in 1532.

Below: Each of the six deity chambers of the Coricancha temples was made with finely dressed stone masonry.

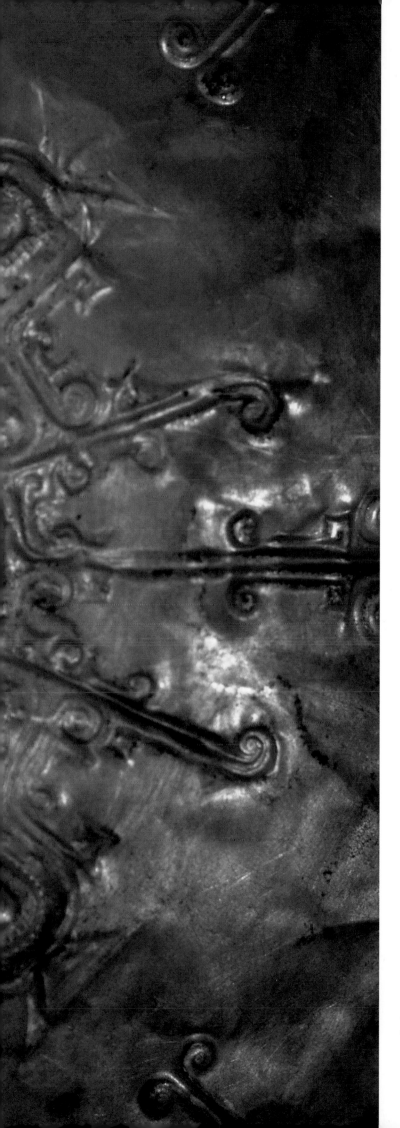

CHAPTER THREE

TALES OF THE GODS

Andean religious beliefs are replete with tales and stories of the deities and their representatives on Earth. However, it is not until the final stages of Andean history that we have this literature, and it is only because the stories were recorded by Spanish chroniclers, priests and administrators from their Inca informants.

These stories concentrate on Inca belief, creation and the rise of the Inca state. Some of the tales hark back to earlier cultures – those collected by the Inca in their conquests. For most of the pre-Inca cultures, however, we have only the archaeological evidence. For the Moche culture in particular, there is a rich 'narrative' of painted scenes on pottery, but most other imagery is of a more static than narrative nature. Nevertheless, an event in progress can be detected in the series of marching figures at Initial Period Cerro Sechín and in the tenoned stone heads on the walls of the temple court at Chavín de Huántar, showing the transformation of a shaman into a jaguar.

The use of creatures from distant, alien environments in the art reveals the contact of cultures across widely dispersed regions. By comparing the images with Inca history and mythological tales, it may be possible to find the origins of belief in pre-Inca cultures. Common imagery, modified through time, inevitably reflects continuity in belief.

Left: The face of the sun god on a gold dish made by a Manteño craftsman (Ecuador) at the far north of the Inca Empire.

SUN GOD AND MOON GODDESS

Ancient Andean traditions link the sun and moon as consorts, the sun being male and the moon female. Both were created and set into motion in the sky by Viracocha, the creator. His association with the sun in particular is made in the east–west orientation of his wanderings. The Islands of the Sun and of the Moon in Lake Titicaca were believed to be their birth places.

There is no doubt that the regular cycles of the sun and moon established recurrent, cyclical ritual calendars in ancient Andean cultures. The association of the sun with celestial matters and the moon with earthly cycles was probably reflected in the first ceremonial architecture – raised platforms symbolizing proximity to the sun and sunken courts providing links to the Earth.

Below: Silver and gold, 'tears of the moon' and 'sweat of the sun', represented an essential Andean duality.

The sun and moon were the epitomy of the Andean concept of duality. As opposites they represented light and dark, warmth and cold. However their importance to life and its everyday cycle was balanced, and thus they achieved oneness through the unity of their cycles.

Neither the Incas nor more ancient Andeans made obvious images of the sun or moon. Faces with radiating appendages are common but cannot be categorically identified as the sun. Images of a crescent moon, however, are found among the pre-Inca northern coastal Moche and Chimú cultures, hinting at a complex mythological tradition now obscure. It may be that the Inca suppressed the Chimú's closer association with the moon by their advocacy of the state cult of Inti, the sun.

AI APAEC AND SI
Among the Moche and Chimú the sky god Ai Apaec was perhaps combined with the sun. He was a somewhat remote and

Above: Niches in the interior of the walls of the Temple of the Moon at Pisac resemble those in the Coricancha in Cuzco.

mysterious creator god who, like Viracocha, paid little attention to the daily affairs of humans. Pictured in art as a fanged deity, his throne was regarded as being the mountaintops. His perception as a sky god appears to be implied by his association with a tableau of two scenes separated by a two-headed serpent. In the upper part appear gods, demonic beings and stars; in the lower part are musicians, lords, or slaves, and rain falling from the serpent's body, implying a celestial and terrestrial division.

Si was the Moche and Chimú moon goddess or god, sometimes regarded as the head of the Moche and Chimú pantheon. He/she was a supreme deity, omnipresent, who held sway over the gods and humankind, and controlled the seasons, natural elements, storms and therefore agricultural fertility. His/her origins can be traced to an un-named radiant and armoured war deity who rivalled or even replaced Ai Apaec in importance among the Chimú. One source refers to a Temple of Si-an dedicated to Si, interpreted as the Huaca Singan in the Jequetepeque Valley, possibly the structure known today as the Huaca del Dragón.

The Moche and Chimú realized that the tides and other motions of the sea, and the arrival of the annual rains, were

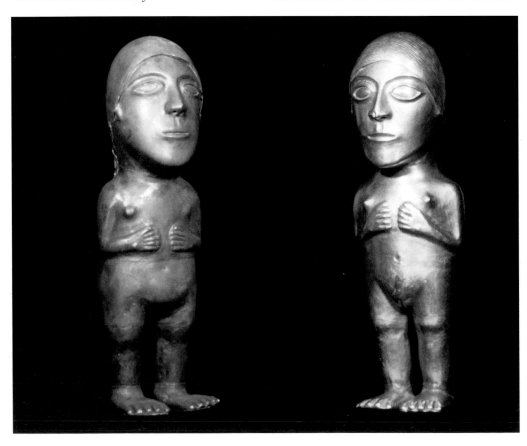

Above: The sacred Intihuatana Temple to Inti the sun god at Pisac, a palace city of Pachacuti Inca Yupanqui, north-east of Cuzco.

linked to the phases of the moon, and thus allocated great power to Si because the food supply and well-being of flocks depended upon his/her beneficence. In contrast, the sun was considered to be a relatively minor deity. Si was regarded as more powerful than the sun because he/she could be seen by both night and day, and eclipses were believed to be battles between the moon and sun. An eclipse of the moon was considered a disastrous augury and regarded with fear; an eclipse of the sun, however, was treated as a joyful occasion.

INTI AND QUILLA
The Incas specifically claimed descent from the sun, but refer less frequently to the moon as their mother, and her role in Inca creation myth is less obvious.

Nevertheless, the chronicler Garcilaso de la Vega describes the moon as sister and wife of the sun, and thus mother of the ancestral Incas.

The Incas worshipped Inti, the sun, but did not frequently portray him. The emperor was regarded as the 'son of the sun' and therefore Inti's embodiment on Earth. They associated the sun with gold, calling it the 'sweat of the sun', and the moon with silver, calling it the 'tears of the moon'. The sun and moon had separate chambers in the Coricancha Temple. The sun was represented by a sheet-gold mask with radiating gold appendages; the moon by a silver image in the shape of a woman.

The solstice days of Capac Raymi (summer/ December) and Inti Raymi (winter/ June) were auspicious days in the Inca ritual calendar.

The Inca empress was regarded as the earthly embodiment of the moon, Quilla, and in her role regulated lunar worship in the capital at Cuzco. A spring moon festival was held in October. An eclipse of the moon was believed by the Incas to be an attempt by a huge celestial serpent or mountain lion to eat Quilla. During such events they would gather in force in their sacred precincts and make as much noise as possible to scare off the creature.

Below: The Temple of the Moon at Machu Picchu was formed from fine masonry and built within a natural rock overhang.

FELINES AND SERPENTS

Feline, serpentine and reptilian imagery pervades Andean religion. Religious animism took the characteristics of such creatures and revered their power, guile and cunning. This was indicative of underlying religious ceremony. Shamans were frequently shown transformed, or transforming, into jaguars or snakes. The cayman was also prominent from early times. The use of feline and reptile imagery also reveals the widespread contacts between cultures that characterized Andean civilization.

Fangs are the most common feature, and they are sometimes indistinct; with claws and a cat-like face, or with a writhing body, the meaning becomes clear. Both images are frequently used in the same compositions.

JAGUARS AND OTHER FELINES

Jaguars and jaguar-humans are universal in the mythology of peoples throughout South America. Among Andean and Pacific coastal cultures the jaguar's face clearly inspired much of the 'fanged god' imagery from the earliest times to the Inca Empire. Its presence confirms the importance of the jungle and of jungle products from the earliest times. Feline creatures were frequently depicted in wall paintings and stone sculpture, and on ceramics, textiles and

Below: A complex row of cayman-like teeth on the cornice at the entrance to the sunken court of the New Temple at Chavín de Huántar.

metalwork. Feline features, especially prominent curved canines, were used on humanoid beings representing shamans and inspired the monster gods of pre-Chavín, Chavín, Moche and Chimú art.

An early example comes from the Initial Period Caballo Muerto Complex in the Moche Valley. The façade of the Huaca de los Reyes two-tiered platform is adorned with six huge, high-relief feline heads, each 2m (6½ft) high, framed within niches. Sculpted in adobe, they have wide feline noses, fangs protruding from drawn-back lips, pendant irises and deep facial

Left: A Late Intermediate Period Chimú wooden jaguar figure, inlaid with bone and mother of pearl, supporting a decorated gourd container.

scarifications – features that influenced later Chavín imagery. They were probably painted.

Jaguar imagery at Chavín de Huántar shows classic shamanic transformation. The Circular Sunken Courtyard within the wings of the U-shaped complex of the Old Temple had two sets of steps descending into it, aligned with the entrance to the central passageway of the temple. The stone-lined walls are made with two strata of large, flat rectangular (lower) and square (upper) slabs, separated by smaller rectangular blocks.

SHAMANIC TRANSFORMATION

The panels are carved in low relief. The upper panels show a parade of composite beings, depicted in profile and many carrying San Pedro hallucinogenic cactus stems. Their stance is human-like but their feet and hands have claws and their grimacing mouths with interlocking fangs show them to be transforming into jaguars. From their headdresses and waists hang snakes, the symbol of spiritual vision. The lower panels form a line of prowling jaguars. Upper and lower panels form

Below: Intertwined desert serpents decorating an Early Intermediate Period Nazca painted bowl.

human-like and animal pairs around the walls. Revealingly, the felines have coat markings that distinguish them as jaguars rather than as highland pumas, with their monochrome coats, and so confirms the mountain–jungle liaison.

The more than 40 tenoned stone heads adorning the New Temple walls of Chavín de Huántar give an equally graphic display of shamanic transformation. They were placed high up, spaced every few metres (yards). Although only one remains *in situ*, reconstruction based on the logic of changes in their features shows them to be a sequence of human to supernatural transformation, from shaman to feline.

Fanged beings remained prominent in the art of later cultures. The Moche Decapitator God has distinctive protruding fangs and double ear-ornaments and the Moche-Chimú sky or creator god Ai Apaec also has a distinctive feline mouth.

SNAKES

Serpentine imagery was as early as feline and, like fanged beasts, was pan-Andean and used in all media: wall paintings, stone carving, ceramic decoration, textiles and metalwork. Snakes feature on the earliest textiles from coastal Preceramic Huaca Prieta, shown in a typical double-meaning composition of snakes and crabs. The combination of a feline head with a serpentine body is also not infrequent.

Initial Period Moxeke has three high-relief, painted adobe sculptures on a 4m (13ft) wide panel on its principal platform. The left and central figures are headless torsos, probably deliberately decapitated; the right-hand sculpture is a colossal head, also probably a decapitation. The two torsos are caped figures, and the central figure has four snakes writhing down its front. The identities are uncertain, but the snakes on the central figure highlight its spiritual role, probably that of a shaman. The composite imagery and presence of snakes are indicative of transformation and spiritual vision. Similar adobe sculptures at Huaca

de los Reyes show human-like figures with snakes hanging from their waists, as do figures in the circular sunken courtyard at Chavín de Huántar described above.

LANZÓN CAYMANS

The Lanzón monolith in the Old Temple at Chavín de Huántar displays many of the features described for later Chavín imagery, but is less specific. It portrays a fantastic beast with a tusked mouth and

Below: A snarling jaguar-faced, bridge-spouted effigy vessel from the Early Intermediate Period Lima culture.

Above: A feline head tops the sinuous serpentine body of an Early Intermediate Period Recuay effigy vessel.

thick, up-turned lips and clawed hands and feet, but is not distinctively feline or reptilian. With only upper fangs, rather than the crossed canines of the jaguars of the circular sunken courtyard, its fanged mouth could have been inspired by several animals. More important is its association with snakes: they adorn its eyebrows, form its hair and dangle from its waistband. Its headdress comprises stacked feline heads, and its waistband is a row of similar feline faces. Significantly, one hand gestures up, the other down, indicating a supreme being whose ruler-ship embraces the universe.

The New Temple Tello Obelisk depicts the creation myth and features two almost identical caymans, identifiable because a cayman's upper row of teeth shows even when its mouth is closed. Additionally, 'flame eyebrows' resemble the heavy brow-ridges, and the form of the legs and feet resemble those of crocodilians. Snakes' heads and other fanged faces also adorn the stone. The dual cayman image represents an early manifestation of duality. The arching figures of 'dragons' at Chimú Huaca del Dragón appear to combine feline, serpentine and celestial elements in a single rainbow-like image.

THE STAFF DEITY

The Staff Deity was the earliest widespread pan-Andean deity. The image originated in the Early Horizon with the Chavín Cult and endured to the Late Intermediate Period. The Staff Deity was portrayed frontally with outstretched arms holding staffs, and could be either male or female. He/she epitomizes the Chavín Cult and the early development of pan-Andean religious belief.

COMPOSITE BEING

Much Chavín imagery was inspired by the natural world. The Staff Deity was a composite human-like being, with male, female or non-distinct genitals. Like other Chavín imagery, the hands and feet end in claws, the mouth displays curved feline fangs, pendant irises hang from the curve of the eyes and the ears are bedecked with all kinds of ornaments. Outstretched arms clutch staffs in one form or another, and they are themselves often festooned with spikes and plume-like decorations. In many cases the staffs held by the Staff Deity are writhing snakes.

THE RAIMONDI STELA

At Chavín de Huántar, the pilgrimage centre of the cult, the most distinctive portrayal of the Staff Deity is undoubtedly the Raimondi Stela (1.98m/6½ft h). Its stylistic similarity to the human-like creatures on the columns of the Black and White Portal of the New Temple suggest that it once stood within one of the New Temple's chambers.

The image on the Raimondi Stela is an incised composition on a highly polished granite-ashlar slab. It has all the hallmarks of the Staff Deity: clawed feet, taloned hands, down-turned, snarling, fanged mouth and pendant irises. Curiously, its genitalia are non-specific. Perhaps, as the most important cult deity at the central cult city, it was meant to represent the unity of opposites (male and female) in order to achieve balance in the Andean worldview.

DUAL MEANING

The Raimondi Stela is not simply a portrait of the Staff Deity. It is an early example of complex, multiple meanings within one image. When viewed as a standing figure, the stela is clearly a Staff Deity wearing an elaborate headdress. The staffs are made up of faces, snakes, vegetation and curved embellishments. Viewed more closely, the headdress comprises similar vegetation, feather-like projections and what appear to be two stacked faces or miniature-bodied standing figures.

This is not all: if the entire image is inverted it shows a different figure. The same principal incised lines of the

Left: A bizarre Staff Deity-like warrior figure on a shallow dish of the Middle Horizon Cajamarca culture of northern Peru.

Above: Andean representations of the Staff Deity in art would be either male or female. This version is male.

Staff Deity face form a new face. What were the irises become nostrils above an upturned, toothy and be-tusked mouth; what were the nostrils of a pug nose become upraised irises; and what were apparent chin dimples beneath the down-turned mouth become the eyes of a grinning face on the forehead of the new face. Finally, the elements that made up the headdress of the Staff Deity image become three sinister-looking faces in which the pendant irises of the headdress faces become nostrils and the new dark areas become widely spaced squinting sets of eyes.

The Staff Deity image appears to be rising, and its various sets of eyes appear to gaze skyward. The inverted features, however, appear to plunge from the sky.

WHO WAS THE STAFF DEITY?

The exact significance and meaning of the Staff Deity is uncertain. His/her power is attested by the number images at Chavín de Huántar on stones and walls, and throughout the central Andes and coast on portable objects. He/she appears to be predominantly associated with agricultural fertility, which is incorporated in the composite features.

The Raimondi Stela image, however, clearly demonstrates aspects of the earliest universals in Andean religion. The profound complexity of the image gives an equally profound religious message of duality within unity.

The celestial orientation of one image and the earthly orientation of the other reveal two deities within one composition. The very viewing point for each of the images points to its respective realm. In context with a platform mound and sunken court at Chavín de Huántar, the

Above: The Raimondi Stela, depicting the supreme deity of the Chavín Cult, can be viewed with meaning either way up.

Above: A female representation of the Staff Deity, showing outstretched arms clasping staffs festooned with decorations.

theme of dual divinity – sky god and earth goddess – was disclosed. Further, the deep recesses of the New Temple secreted meaning and divided worshippers into inclusive and exclusive groups.

AN ENDURING DEITY

The Staff Deity's potency is likewise demonstrated by endurance. The imagery is interrupted in the Late Intermediate Period, but early colonial depictions of the Inca kings show them holding a staff in each hand. Such exceptional importance through longevity imbues the Staff Deity with a distinct 'personality' and the supernatural power of an early creator god.

Chavín Staff Deity images were found everywhere throughout central Andean and Pacific coastal sites in the Early Horizon, on stone sculptures, ceramics and textiles. Of particular note are the Staff Deity images painted on cotton textiles from the Karwa culture of the Paracas Peninsula. There are more than 25 of them, all clearly female. Appendages of cotton growing from the staffs and headdress symbolize the principal agriculture of the coast, and perhaps reveal her to be wife or consort of the Chavín deity, in a locally focused cult.

The most prominent Middle Horizon representation of the Staff Deity is the central figure on the monumental portal at Tiwanaku. Staff Deity images are frequent in both Tiwankau and Wari art.

MUMMIFICATION AND THE OCULATE BEING

The Paracas culture of southern coastal Peru was one of the first Andean cultures to practise mummification. Great reverence is shown by the elaborate preparation of the bodies. The mummies were 'bundled' in tight, foetal positions, placed in baskets and wrapped in layers of high-quality cotton and llama-wool textiles displaying a wealth of natural imagery and supernatural iconography – a rich mythology associated with ritual practices. The burials were accompanied by decorated and plain pottery, many in the shapes of animal effigies, and by sheet-gold ornaments. The freshness of the textiles indicates they were made specifically for burial. Some pieces were even unfinished before needed!

Above: In this woven example, a human-like Oculate Being has whiskers, eyes with pupils, a golden diadem headpiece, and trophy heads.

Among and between sprawling areas of habitation, special necropolis sites had been chosen for hundreds of burials. These might have been the foci of family cults. As the numbers of burials appear to exceed the needs of the immediately adjacent settlements, it is thought that the Paracas necropolises might also have been pilgrimage centres for a regional cult, with honoured individuals being brought from more distant settlements for burial.

A LOCAL DEITY

The Paracas style was heavily influenced by the Chavín style of the north-central Andes, but had soon developed its own regional flavour. Without written records we can only surmise the names and details of Paracas deities and ceremonial practices. Fanged creatures – highly stylized feline faces – feature frequently on textiles and ceramics, but among them one is especially prominent: the Oculate Being.

Left: The Nazca inherited the Paracas Oculate Being. In this rather stylized version, the Oculate Being is shown with his essential feature: blank, staring eyes.

The Oculate Being was most often portrayed horizontally on textiles and ceramics, as if flying, often upside-down (perhaps looking down on humankind), and crouching. With no distinctively female attributes, 'he' is assumed to be male. He has a characteristic, frontal face with large, circular, staring eyes – hence the name. Long, streaming appendages originate from various parts of his body and end in trophy heads or small figures.

He is depicted on textiles and pots, and in the form of distinctive ceramic masks brightly painted with his countenance. Significantly, the Oculate Being is the only image shown on these masks, a fact, it is argued, that emphasizes his importance as a regional deity. His face is often heart-shaped on pottery and in textiles, and sometimes sprouts a smaller head from its top. On other figures, he wears a headband identical to sheet-gold headbands found in some Paracas burials.

SHAMANS AND SERPENTS

Dilated eyes are characteristic of shamanic vision, perhaps inspired by the perceived powers of the round, reflective eyes of nocturnal animals. Numerous birds are depicted in Paracas and Nazca art, in all media, and it is not surprising that the owl was known in later Andean religion as an alter-ego of the shaman.

Despite his regional ownership, the Oculate Being employs the universal Andean iconography of the serpent. Flying Oculate Beings often have long, trailing serpentine tongues; on one textile, two images share a tongue, forming a duality. They often wear writhing belts of snakes trailing behind their legs, demonstrating a sense of artistic perspective. Oculate Being masks have undulating double-headed snakes across the face; on some such masks the forehead snake forms the arms of the miniature figure on the brow, and the figure itself also has a serpent across its forehead.

Above: Here the Oculate Being is shown several times inside a ceramic bowl with typical feline attributes, serpentine tongue, snakes and sky symbols.

DECAPITATION

There are also indications of ritual decapitation. One textile shows a group of flying Oculate Beings each carrying a crescent-shaped knife typical of the *tumi* shape known to be used for decapitation, especially among the Moche, Lambayeque (Sicán) and Chimú cultures of the Early Intermediate to Late Intermediate Periods. Other images of the Oculate Being show him holding a staff, not in a frontal stance with two staffs, like the Staff Deity of the Chavín Cult, but still possibly inspired by Chavín iconography. Later Paracas textiles show the Oculate Being more stylistically, owing partly to the use of a new weaving technique known as discontinuous warp and weft.

In the Early Intermediate Period, the Oculate Being cult continued to form an important part of the art images of the succeeding Nazca culture in the same region. One Nazca painted textile shows figures facing forwards and holding agricultural products. Their visages appear bespectacled and they have strange flaring moustaches and beards. One holds a mask. Another painted textile, known as the 'Harvest Festival', shows a crowded scene of little figures, facing front, with outstretched arms holding agricultural produce. Their stances resemble the Staff Deity, while their faces have the wide-eyed stare characteristic of the Oculate Being or of shamanic trance.

THE MEANING OF THE BEING

The role of the Oculate Being is difficult to determine. His round visage, association with flying and burial, and depiction with decapitation knives all indicate attributes of a god of the sun, sky, death or sacrifice. With such combined characteristics, perhaps he was an early manifestation of the supreme deity. The relationship between the Oculate Being and the Chavín Staff Deity is equally unknown, despite the appearance of unmistakeable Chavín influence at Karwa, just south of the Paracas cemeteries.

THE DECAPITATOR GOD

In a diamond frame, the grimacing face of a fearsome-looking half-human, half-jaguar peers from the walls of Platform I and the Great Plaza of the Huaca de la Luna at Moche. Stylized, stepped supernatural faces surround it, linked by a common 'thread' as if woven in textile. The face is outlined in red. Black hair and a beard curl from the head and chin. A sausage-shaped, down-turned mouth snarls, displaying human-like rows of white teeth and interlocked feline canines. His ears appear to be pierced and decorated with double ear-ornaments. Huge white eyes underlined in black and with heavy red brows stare menacingly with large black pupils. Curious, alien-looking miniature faces surround the head. This mural depicts the Decapitator God. What fear and reverence might he have struck in citizens as they stood beneath his gaze watching priests perform ritual sacrifice?

Below: Murals at the Huaca de la Luna depict a wide-eyed shamanic face with pierced ears, human teeth and feline canines.

RITUAL BLOOD-LETTING

The Decapitator God so graphically dominating the Moche capital was depicted in friezes and murals in temples and tombs, and on ceramics and metalwork at Moche and other north coastal valley sites, including Sipán in the Lambayeque Valley. He has several guises: as an overpowering face that grips one's attention, or full-figured, holding a crescent-shaped *tumi* ceremonial knife in one hand and a severed human head in the other. The elaborate plaster friezes at the Huaca de la Luna of Early Intermediate Period Moche are the most renowned, but the development of his imagery can be traced back to the Early Horizon in the preceding Cupisnique culture of the same region.

The Decapitator God is portrayed in an elaborate blood-letting rite painted on pottery and on temple and tomb walls. His role, acted out by priests, embodied

Above: There is no mistaking this sheet-metal and shell inlay depiction of the Decapitator God, with his grinning sinister expression, tumi *sacrificial knife and his latest victim's head.*

a gruesome sacrificial ritual. Although once thought to be merely representational of a mythical event, archaeological evidence discovered in the 1980s attests to its reality. An enclosure behind the Huaca de la Luna platform contained the buried remains of 40 men, aged 15 to 30. They appear to have been pushed off a stone outcrop after having been mutilated and killed. The structure, outcrop and enclosure seem to mirror the nearby Cerro Blanco and valley. Some skeletons were splayed out as if tied to stakes; some had their femurs torn from the pelvis joints; skulls, ribs, fingerbones, armbones and legbones have cut marks. Several severed heads had their jaws torn away.

A thick layer of sediment, deposited during heavy rains, covered the gruesome scene, and it is suggested that the sacrifice was performed in response to an El Niño event that might have disrupted the economic stability of the realm.

RITUAL COMBAT

The Decapitator God and sacrificial ritual are put into context by scenes painted on Moche ceramics and walls. Friezes show warriors in paired combat, almost always both wearing Moche armour and bearing Moche arms. The combatants are shown in narrative sequences: instead of killing a vanquished foe, the loser is next shown stripped and tied by the neck with a rope, being marched off for their arraignment. The final scenes show the captives naked, having their throats slit. Their blood is given in goblets to four presiding figures.

The most elaborate of these is the Warrior Priest. He wears a crescent-shaped metal plate to protect his back, and rattles hang from his belt. To his right sits the Bird Priest, wearing a conical helmet bearing the image of an owl and a long beak-like nose-ornament. Next to him is a priestess, identified by her long, plaited tresses, dress-like costume and plumed and tasselled headdress. The final figure, with a feline face, wears a headdress with serrated border and long streamers.

THE REAL THING

These scenes show ritual warfare in fields near Moche cities for the purpose of 'capturing' victims for sacrifices to the gods. Excavations in the 1980s of unlooted Sipán tombs in the Lambayeque Valley dated c.AD300 corroborate their actual occurrence. The elite citizens buried in the tombs, accompanied by sacrificial victims, were richly adorned and surrounded by the artefacts of sacrifice and ritual; the bodies were decorated with gold, silver, turquoise and other jewellery, and textiles. They wore

Right: A Chimú gold sacrificial knife handle, representing the legendary leader and conqueror Naymlap.

costumes identical to those of the four figures in the sacrificial ceremonies.

The principal body personifies the Warrior Priest. He wore a crescent-shaped back-flap and belt rattles, just as in the scene. The Decapitator God image decorates both back-flap and rattles – in this case the face is symbolized by a spider with a human face, perched on a golden web. The spider imagery is thought to reflect the parallel of the blood-letting and sucking the life juices of its prey. Offerings included three pairs of gold and turquoise ear-spools – one of which shows a Moche warrior in full armour – a gold, crescent-shaped headdress, a crescent-shaped nose-ornament, and one gold and one silver *tumi* knife. At the Warrior Priest's side lay a box-like gold sceptre, embossed with combat scenes, and a spatula-like handle of silver studded with military trappings.

Near by, another tomb, less rich, contained the body of a noble with a gilded copper headdress decorated with an owl with outspread wings – clearly the Bird Priest. Scaled rectangular rooms near the tombs contained more offerings, including the bones of severed human hands and feet.

Two tombs dated c.AD 500–600 at San José de Moro in the Jequetepeque Valley contained the skeletons of women. Their silver-alloyed copper headdresses had tassels and other accoutrements of the priestess figure. Finally, at El Brujo in the Chicama Valley, a terrace frieze shows a life-size warrior leading a procession of ten nude prisoners by a rope placed around their necks. On a terrace above (later destroyed by looters) was a huge spider or crab with a fanged mouth and double ear-ornaments, one leg brandishing a *tumi* knife – the 'arachnoid decapitator'.

CON THE CREATOR

Con created and shaped the natural world, made the first generation of humans and gave life to the animals and plants. He is central in a generic creation myth, but is not always benevolent. His name forms part of other Andean creator deities such as Con Tici (or Titi) Viracocha Pachayachachic, Coniraya Viracocha of the early 17th-century *Huarochirí Manuscript*, and Wakon. The word 'con' is indicative of heat, energy and creation.

CON VERSUS PACHACAMAC

Con was a formless figure, without bones or joints, who came from the north and was a child of the sun and the moon. After walking up and down the coast, shaping the land and creating all things in it, he disappeared into the sea and ascended into the sky.

The central Andean Colloas believed that Con created the sun, then made stone figures of the various Andean peoples, whom he placed throughout the valleys before bringing them to life and instructing them in his worship.

Con's rival or opposite was Pachacamac. Because he had left the world's inhabitants without a leader or protector, Pachacamac, who came from the south, transformed these first humans into pumas/jaguars, foxes, monkeys and parrots.

WAKON AND THE SPIDER

In a later tradition, Wakon was a malevolent being opposed to Pachacamac, who, with his consort Pacha Mama, were sky and earth deities respectively. Their union produced twins, a boy and a girl, after which Pachacamac died and disappeared into the sea, leaving Pacha Mama and the twins alone.

Wakon, who lived in a cave, appeared semi-naked to the twins. He asked them to fetch some water and while they were away seduced Pacha Mama. He ate part of her and threw the rest of her body into a cooking pot. When the twins returned and learned of her fate, they fled. Wakon asked

Above: A puma-headed reed boat on Lake Titicaca on whose shore the survivors from the flood landed.

the animals and birds where the twins were hiding. Spider suggested that he go to a mountaintop and call to the twins, imitating Pacha Mama's voice. Spider, however, had prepared a trap, a chasm on the mountain, into which Wakon fell and was destroyed, causing a violent earthquake. Pachacamac then returned, apologized to the twins and transformed his son into the

sun and his daughter into the moon. Pacha Mama 'survived' as the snow-capped mountain La Viuda (the widow).

In later myths, Con became blended with Viracocha. The central Andean Cachas, for example, called him Con Tici Viracocha Pachayachachic, literally 'god, creator of the world'.

CON TICI OF THE TIWANAKU

In one version of the Inca creation myth, related by the 16th-century chronicler Cristobal de Molina, the world was already peopled when a great flood destroyed all except one man and one woman. They were cast up on land at Tiwanaku, where Con Tici Viracocha appeared to them and created a second race of humans of clay and stone in the Titicaca Basin, including the Inca ancestors. He also made birds and animals, two of each, and spread them among their habitats, designated their foods, and gave each bird its song.

He named two of his creations (sometimes said to be his sons) Imaymana Viracocha and Tocapo Viracocha, the inclusion of 'Viracocha' imbuing them with divinity and supernatural power. With them he travelled throughout the land giving life to the peoples, animals and plants that he had created. Imaymana Viracocha went north-westwards along the forest and mountain borders, Tocapo Viracocha went northwards along the coasts, and Con Tici Viracocha went along a route between them,

Below: Con/Viracocha, the bodiless or formless deity, is appropriately represented in this blocky, rather abstract form.

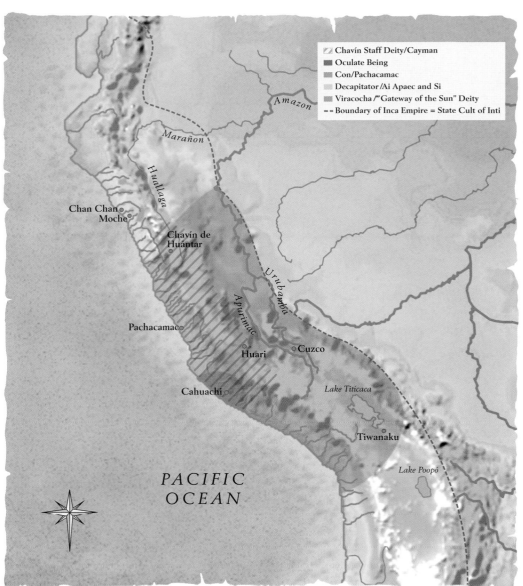

Above: Map showing the distribution of the major creator deities, from the Decapitator in the north to the Oculate Being in the south.

through the mountains. They continued to what became the north-westernmost edge of the Inca Empire, to the coastal site of Manta, where they walked out across the sea until they disappeared.

Coniraya Viracocha of central Andean Huarochirí mythology, like Con, was a coastal creator deity who wandered throughout the world, reshaping the landscape before disappearing across the western sea. Like Wakon, Coniraya sought Pachacamac's children by asking the animals and birds about them.

HISTORY BEHIND A MYTH?
The conflict between Con and Pachacamac might represent the later mythologizing of historical consciousness, a shared general memory of past events in a culture without written records. In the versions related above, Con comes from either north or south, and travels up and down the coasts,

mountains and forests. From the north, he would have represented a Moche or earlier deity of the northern coastal valleys. It has also been suggested that the shapeless Con is represented by the flying human-like sky deities on the textiles and pottery of the Paracas and Nazca peoples of the southern coasts, and continued as the winged attendants associated with the Staff Deity at Tiwanaku. Together, these cultures span the Early Horizon, Early Intermediate Period and Middle Horizon.

The conflict between them and the replacement of Con by Pachacamac would thus reflect the decline of southern cults and the rise of the importance of middle coastal Pachacamc as a deity, and of his associated temple and pilgrimage cult.

THE YAYA-MAMA RELIGIOUS TRADITION

A tall stone post from Taraco on the northern shore of Lake Titicaca is carved on all four faces. Two opposite faces have a male and a female figure, giving the name Yaya-Mama – father and mother – to a regional cult. Below each figure, and on the other two faces, there are writhing serpents. Three of the four serpents on the faces adjacent to the figured faces are double-headed.

A REGIONAL CULT

Pukará, another Yaya-Mama site north of the lake, flourished as a regional cult centre in the late Early Horizon and Early Intermediate Period, before the rise of the Wari and Tiwanaku states to the north and south. Yaya-Mama developed independently of the Chavín Cult to the north, and provided the template for later south-central Andean civilization. Tiwanaku people revered the Yaya-Mama tradition, as evidenced by their incorporation of Yaya-Mama sculptures in their own ceremonial complexes. For example, Yaya-Mama Stela 15 (2m/6½ft high) was erected beside the much taller Bennett Monolith (7.4m/24ft high) in the Semi-subterranean Temple at Tiwanaku; and the lower part of the Arapa-Thunderbolt Stela was taken from Arapa, at the north end of the lake, and placed in the Putuni Palace at Tiwanku. Altogether there are a total of seven Pukará sculptures at the city of Tiwanaku.

Above: At Lake Titicaca the cult of Yaya-Mama/Pukará was established at ceremonial centres around the lake.

Pukará stone sculpture is blocky and columnar. Its imagery features flat, squared-oval eyes. Movement is indicated in the poses and limbs of figures, and ribs show prominently. Hands sometimes hold objects. Heads are frequently rayed with feathers and animal images emanating from the main heads. As well as monumental stone sculpture, there were roofless temples and sunken courts, complex supernatural artistic symbols and ritual paraphernalia.

Dozens of Pukará temple sites are distributed more or less equidistantly around Lake Titicaca, located on hill summits, on artificial platforms and at the bases of cliffs. Yaya-Mama temples typically comprise a rectangular sunken court, which is surrounded by individual, multi-chambered structures arranged symmetrically around the court. The

Left: Pukará ceramics shared features that resemble later Tiwanaku styles in the use of incised decoration and colours.

courts are stone lined, either plain or carved with heads that have appendages radiating from them. Sometimes there are burials around the court.

A TWO-PHASED TRADITION

Most Yaya-Mama stone sculptures have not been found *in situ*. Some are still objects of local veneration. Lasting about a millennium, the style comprises two phases, characterized by examples from Chiripa (earlier) and Pukará (later). Earlier pieces are mostly pecked designs of geometric symbols, animals and humans on stone slabs or four-sided posts. Later examples are incised and carved in the round, showing greater finishing. Generally, human figures are carved in the round while animals and geometric motifs are in low relief.

Early Yaya-Mama stone imagery shows pairs of figures, male and female, with arms raised to their chests. Human heads have appendages radiating from them that often end in triangular serpent heads. There are also severed human heads.

Above: The characteristic Pukará-style Yaya-Mama features a life-size or larger stone head with a turban-like headdress.

Animals include felines, birds with outstretched wings, frogs and/or toads, snakes, or supernatural serpentine creatures with flared ears and zigzag bodies. Geometric designs include checkered and Maltese-like crosses, chevrons and rings.

The most common animal on pottery is the spotted feline – the spotted coat indicating the jaguar rather than the monochrome mountain lion. There are also trophy heads and dismembered sacrificial victims, birds, coiled snakes and camalids. The characteristic vertical division of eyes into black and white halves of Tiwanaku and Wari imagery is first seen in Pukará art, as are tears below the eyes.

Later Pukará stone sculptures feature large slabs carved with felines, coiled snakes, frogs and/or toads, steps, volutes and zigzags. Humans are carved in the round. There are seated and standing males figures, one wearing a serpent-head decorated hat. The Pukará Decapitator depicts a seated male figure, holding an axe in his right hand and a severed head in his left. His cap is decorated with supernatural faces. He is either a supernatural composite being, or a man wearing a representative mask with a fanged mouth. The round, staring eyes are indicative of shamanic trance or transformation.

RITUAL PARAPHERNALIA

Yaya-Mama ritual paraphernalia includes ceremonial burners, ceramic and *Strombus* shell trumpets, miniature pottery vessels, including painted and effigy-shaped pieces, and architectural models. Pottery vessels are invariably found in pieces and contexts that indicate deliberate breakage.

Two prominent ceramic themes are the 'feline man' and the 'woman with alpaca'. The first depicts pairs of fanged men lunging forward or running, facing each other or one chasing the other. Each figure carries a severed head and a staff. Some figures wear feline pelts. The 'woman with alpaca' shows a single, skirted, frontal-standing figure leading an alpaca by a rope. She carries a bag and holds a distinctive staff with an I-shaped head, and she wears a plumed cap. She is associated with plants and sometimes a rayed-head motif.

From the Pukará temple come rectangular stone boxes, subdivided and externally decorated on six equal panels with stylized faces, each with 16 appendages ending in a variety of serpent or circular heads. Ceramic models are of miniature temples, complete with the details of their windows and doors.

These objects and images imply ritual combat, agricultural and pastoral themes, and fertility. Ritual clearly included incense burning, feasting and music-making. Images of severed heads – a feature of religious symbolism throughout the Andean Area – and dismembered bodies, and a cache of human mandibles found at Pukará, indicate ritual sacrifice and/or warfare, either in the real world or in the world of mythological concept.

Below: Accurate, individual and natural features are complemented by ringed/lidded eyes, but without pupils.

VIRACOCHA: THE SUPREME ANDEAN DEITY

Viracocha was the supreme deity, almost universally regarded throughout the Andean Area as the creator of the universe, the human race and all living things. He became a rather remote and inaccessible deity, although regarded as omnipresent and inescapable.

In Cuzco he was represented in his own shrine by a golden statue slightly smaller than life. He was white, bearded and wore a long tunic, as described by the Spaniards who first saw him there. In Inca legend, he travelled south to Cacha, *c.*100km (60 miles) south of Cuzco, where another temple and statue were dedicated to his worship. Another shrine and statue were at Urcos.

THE PRIMORDIAL CREATOR

To the Incas, Viracocha was primordial. He remained nameless, and instead was referred to by descriptive terms befitting his role in the various permutations of the creation myth. He was Illya ('light'), Tici ('the beginning of things'), Atun Viracocha ('great creator), or Viracocha Pachayachachic ('lord, instructor of the world'). The earliest Spanish chroniclers to describe him, Cieza de León and Juan de Betanzos around 1550, personify him, but to ancient Andeans 'he' represented a concept – the force of creative energy. The Quechua elements of his name, *vira* ('fat, grease, foam') and *cocha* ('lake, sea, reservoir'), can be rendered as 'sea fat', 'sea foam', or 'the lake of creation'.

As supreme deity, Viracocha's name has been used for the creator god in the pantheons of many pre-Inca cultures. Much of his history and legend therefore owes to the Inca's adoption of him from their conquered subjects. For example, his portrayal with weeping eyes was a characteristic almost certainly adopted from the weeping god imagery of Tiwanaku. In Inca legend he bestowed a special headdress and stone battle-axe on Manco Capac, the first Inca ruler, and prophesied that the Incas would become

great lords and would conquer many other nations. Viracocha Inca, the 15th-century eighth Inca ruler, took his name, presumably as representing strength and creative energy. As a concept, he could also be regarded as 'shapeless' or 'boneless'.

CREATION AND LAKE TITICACA

Many Andean cultures believed that Lake Titicaca was where the sun, moon and stars were created, and that the lake waters were the tears of Viracocha acknowledging the sufferings of his creations.

Viracocha first created a world of darkness, then populated it with humans fashioned from stone. But he was disobeyed, so he destroyed them with a flood or by transforming them back into stones. These beings could be seen, it was

Above: Viracocha came to be associated with other sky symbols such as the double-headed rainbow serpent found in Chimú art.

thought, at ruined cities such as Tiwanaku and Pukará. Only one man and one woman survived, and were magically transported to Tiwanaku, where the gods dwelled.

Viracocha next created a new race of humans, and animals, of clay. He painted distinctive clothes on the humans and gave them customs, languages, songs, arts and crafts, and the gift of agriculture to distinguish the different peoples and nations. Breathing life into them, he instructed them to descend into the earth and disperse, then to re-emerge through caves, and from lakes and hills. These places became sacred, and shrines were established at them in honour of the gods.

The world was still dark, so Viracocha ordered the sun, moon and stars to rise into the sky from the islands in Lake Titicaca.

SPREADING CIVILIZATION

After his creations, Viracocha set out from the Titicaca Basin to spread civilization, but he did so as a beggar, bearded, dressed in rags, and under many names, and dependant on others for his sustenance. In other accounts he was described as a tall white man wearing a sun crown. Many of those he encountered reviled him. He was assisted by two of his creations, variously called his sons or brothers: Imaymana Viracocha and Tocapo Viracocha. The inclusion of the name 'Viracocha' imbued them with divinity and supernatural power.

He commanded Imaymana Viracocha to travel north-westward along a route bordering the forests and mountains and Tocapo Viracocha to journey northward along a coastal route. He himself followed a route between them, north-westward through the mountains. As they passed

Below: Temples were dedicated to Viracocha throughout the Inca Empire, as here at Rachi in the Vilcanota Valley.

through the land, they called out the people, named the trees and plants, established the times when each would flower and bear fruit, and instructed the people about which were edible and which medicinal. They taught humankind the arts and crafts, agriculture and the ways of civilization, and worked miracles among them, until they reached Manta on the Ecuadorian coast (the most north-

Above: A portrayal of Viracocha's face in sheet gold features typical Tiwanaku sun rays around the head, and weeping eyes.

western edge of the Inca Empire), where they continued across the sea, walking on the water until they disappeared.

Another version, recorded by Cristobal de Molina, begins with the world already peopled. A great flood destroyed all except one man and one woman, who were cast up on land at Tiwanaku. Con Tici Viracocha appeared to them and ordered them to remain there as *mitimaes* (people resettled by the Incas), then repopulated the land by making the Inca ancestors out of clay, and as before, giving them customs, languages and clothing.

This active role on Earth likens Viracocha to the preacher heroes in much pre-Inca legend. To the Incas, Viracocha remained remote, interacting with humans through other gods, particularly Inti, the sun god, and Illapa, god of weather. His purposeful travels relate to ancient Andean pilgrimage traditions. The trinity implied by the three Viracochas suggests a strong element of Christian interpretation in the descriptions of the Spanish chroniclers.

PACHACAMAC THE CREATOR

Pachacamac, 'earth/time maker', was the creator deity of the peoples of the central Peruvian coast. His Quechua root words, *pacha* ('time/space', 'universe/earth', 'state of being') and *camac* ('creator', 'animator') render him as potent as Viracocha and reveal lowland–highland association through the spread of Quechua from coastal regions to the Andes.

AN ANCIENT ORACLE

The centre of Pachacamac's worship was the pilgrimage city and oracle of the same name near modern Lima. The 16th-century chronicler Cieza de León noted Inca reverence for the shrine, and the 17th-century writer Father Bernabe Cobo describes it in detail. The Earth Maker was represented by a wooden staff (destroyed by Hernando Pizarro, brother of the conquistador) carved with a human face on both sides and housed in an oracular chamber, epitomizing the Andean concept of duality. Other carved wooden idols, which were scattered about the city, survive from other parts of the site.

Below: For more than a millennium, complexes of courtyards at Pachacamac accommodated pilgrims.

Pachacamac's following was ancient and widespread among central coastal civilizations, enduring from the Early Intermediate Period for more than a millennium. The oracle, like Early Horizon Chavín de Huántar, drew visitors from throughout the lowland plains and valleys, and the adjacent Andes. The principal temple platform was surrounded by a vast complex of courtyards and subsidiary platforms for the accommodation of pilgrims. Like Lake Titicaca and the Coricancha in Cuzco, it was one of the most sacred sites in the Inca Empire.

THE CREATION MYTH

There are many threads to Pachacamac's mythology. He was a serious rival to Viracocha. His cult developed independently and much earlier than that of Inca Inti, but the predominance of ancient contact between the coastal lowlands and the Andean highlands inevitably brought the two creator gods into 'contact' at an early date, long before the Inca compulsion to incorporate all their subjects' myths and pantheons of gods.

Mythology shows the two deities to have distinct identities, yet many similar traits: they created the world; they held control over the creation and destruction of the

Above: Guaman Poma de Ayala's depiction of a child sacrifice to Pachacamac in his Nueva Crónica y Buen Gobierno, *c.1613.*

first people; they travelled throughout the lands and taught, often in the guise of a beggar, and punished those who mocked them for this; they met, named, and gave their characters to the animals and plants.

In the principal myth, Pachacamac was the son of the sun and moon. An earlier deity, Con, had created the first people, but Pachacamac overcame him, and transformed the first people into monkeys and other animals.

Pachacamac then created man and woman, but, because he did not provide them with food, the man died. The woman solicited the sun's help, or in another version accused the sun of neglecting his duty, and in return was impregnated by the sun's rays. When she bore a son, she taught him to survive by eating wild plants. Pachacamac, jealous of his father (the sun) and angered by this independence and apparent defiance, killed the boy and cut him into pieces. He sowed the boy's teeth, which grew into maize; planted the ribs and bones, which became yucca, or manioc, tubers; and planted the flesh, which grew

into vegetables and fruits. The story appears to be a mythical précis of the discovery of cultivation among coastal peoples.

Not to be outdone, the sun took the boy's penis (or umbilical cord) and navel and created another son, whom he named Vichama or Villama. Pachacamac wanted to kill this child too, but could not catch him, for Vichama had set off on his travels. Pachacamac slew the woman instead and fed her body to the vultures and condors.

Next, Pachacamac created another man and woman, who began to repopulate the world. Pachacamac appointed some of these people *curacas* (leaders) to rule.

In the mean time, Vichama returned, found his mother's remains and reassembled her. Pachacamac feared Vichama's reprisal as the pursued became the pursuer, and he was driven, or fled, into the sea, where he sank in front of the temple of Pachacamac/Vichama. Wreaking further revenge, Vichama transformed Pachacamac's second people into stone, but later repented and changed the ordinary stone of the *curacas* into sacred *huacas*.

Below: The Incas established a temple to Inti (the sun god) alongside the ancient platform at Pachacamac.

SOCIAL ARRANGEMENTS

The second part of the tale explains the creation of social order among humans. Vichama asked his father, the sun, to create another race of people. The sun sent three eggs, one gold, one silver and one copper. The gold egg became *curacas* and nobles, the silver became women, and the copper egg became commoners. Thus, the world was populated. A variation describes how Pachacamac did the final deed by sending four stars to earth. Two of these were male, and generated kings and nobles; the other two were female, and generated commoners.

Other variations combine Con and Viracocha, emphasizing the latter's opposition to Pachacamac. The Huarochirí, between coast and sierra, incorporate Pachacamac's shrine, wife and daughters (including the seduction and attempted seduction of Pachacamac's daughters) into the itinerary of Coniriya Viracocha.

Such variations reflect lowland–highland and inter-coastal exchange and political tension. In the interests of empire, the Incas sought to alleviate any potential conflict by amalgamating the deities and by presenting variations as different names for the same events, as if it had always been so.

Above: Pachacamac was principally a coastal creator god who was ultimately combined with Viracocha, the highland creator deity.

INTI THE SUN GOD

The solstices were crucial days in the Inca ritual calendar. At Capac Raymi (summer/December), there was an imperial feast and initiation rites for noble boys; Inti Raymi (winter/June) honoured Inti, the sun, with feasting and the taking of important auguries. Plotting and confirming their dates was based on observations from the sacred Coricancha Temple in Cuzco.

THE CULT OF INTI

In Inca belief the sun was set in the sky by Viracocha, creator being of indistinct substance. The founding Inca ancestor, Manoc Capac, was believed to have been descended from the sun – the son of the sun – and this belief began the special relationship between the Incas and Inti. The adoption of the cult of Inti was associated especially with the ninth ruler, Pachacuti. Inca imperial expansion probably introduced a solar element into the mythologies of coastal peoples, as the father of Con and Pachacuti. Thus began the combining of creation myths with Inti, the sun.

Inti's image was most frequently a great sheet-gold mask, moulded as a human-like face, wide-eyed and showing a toothy grin. Sheet-gold rays, cut in zig-zags and ending in miniature human-like masks or figures, surrounded the face. Rayed faces were a common feature of pre-Inca

Below: The Christian Church of Santo Domingo, superimposed on the Coricancha Temple, dedicated in part to Inti.

Above: Llamas were frequently sacrificed to honour Inti, as depicted in this colonial painting of a sacrificial ceremony.

imagery, but their identification as the sun is not always tenable.

The sacred Coricancha precinct in Cuzco was the centre of the official state cult dedicated to Inti's worship. By the 16th century, the cult of Inti was so important that an incident witnessed by the priests during ceremonies in his honour appeared to foretell the fall of the empire. An eagle, mobbed by buzzards, was seen falling from the sky in the reign of Huayna Capac about 1526, coinciding with reports of the spread of an unknown, deadly disease from the north, now known to have been smallpox.

CAPTURING THE SUN

The emperor was seen as Inti's embodiment on Earth. Although regarded with awe because of his power, Inti was believed to be benevolent and generous. The sun was symbolically captured at special locations called *intihuatanas* ('hitching posts of the sun'), for example at Machu Picchu – carved stone outcrops probably used for astronomical observations. Together with set stone pillars,

priests used the shadows cast by them to observe and record regular movements of the sun in order to understand it and to predict the future. Solar eclipses were regarded as signs of Inti's anger.

INTERMEDIARIES

By the second half of the 15th century, as the empire reached the limits of expansion, Viracocha had become a remote deity, and Inti came to be regarded as his intermediary. Inca rulers emphasized this relationship carefully, and it became the basis for cultivating their intimate association with Inti. They became intermediaries between the sun and the people, and their presence was regarded as essential to assure light and warmth to make the world habitable. Elaboration and adoption of regional mythologies and combining them with Inca myth created an association between Inti, the emperor and power. Ceremonies and ritual offerings to Inti served constantly to reinforce this link.

Above: Perhaps the most celebrated intihuatana *is the one located at the highest point of the sacred city of Machu Picchu.*

THE RIGHT TO RULE

Historical and archaeological evidence shows that the expansion of the Inca empire beyond the Cuzco Valley began in earnest with Pachacuti Inca Yupanqui (1438–71) and with his son Tupac Yupanqui (1471–93). To unify the empire and convince their subjects of the Inca right to rule it became necessary to demonstrate a mythical common ancestry – namely the Inca ancestors. Thus, the first ruler, Manco Capac (at first called Ayar Manco), after emerging from the cave of Tambo Toco, acquired divine sanction when his brother Ayar Uchu flew up and spoke to the sun. Ayar Uchu returned with the message that Manco should thenceforth rule Cuzco as Manco Capac in the name of the sun.

Other versions of the creation myth name Inti as the father of Ayar Manco Capac and Mama Coya (also Mama Ocllo), and the other brother/sister/partners collectively known as the ancestors. Manco Capac and Mama Ocllo were sent to Earth to bring the gifts of maize and potato cultivation, establishing the Inca right to rule on the basis of their benevolence.

Below: The Intihuatana *or Hitching Post of the Sun at Machu Picchu was probably used for astronomical observations.*

A somewhat more sinister variation says that 'son of the sun' (Inti) was the nickname given to Manco Capac by his father to trick the populace of Cuzco into handing over power. Manco Capac wore gold plates to lend credulity to his divine dawn appearance to the people of Cuzco.

The emperor Pachacuti Inca Yupanqui's discovery of the crystal tablet in the spring of Susurpuquio, with its image of Viracocha, was followed by renewed construction and rearrangement of the sacred Coricancha, giving greater prominence to Inti. It was Pachacuti, too, who visited the Island of the Sun in Lake Titicaca, where ancient Andeans believed the sun to have been born. The construction of Sacsahuaman, at the north-west end of the capital, was probably also begun by Pachacuti. It became a sacred precinct and place of sacrifice to Inti, and probably also a site for cosmological observations. All these legendary events enhanced the importance of Inti and therefore the Incas.

CHAPTER FOUR

CREATION AND THE FIRST PEOPLES

The creation story of the Ancient Andean peoples involved a layered world that revolved in endless cycles of creation and rebirth. They linked these concepts to their intimate association with their landscape to explain both its bounty and the difficulties and trials it sometimes presented.

The Spaniards recorded a wealth of rival, even seemingly contradictory, tales of creation among the peoples of the Inca Empire – and indeed throughout their New World colonies. However, as among the cultures of Mesoamerica, Andean cultural accounts of cosmic origin and the creation of humankind had common elements that arose from a long and common inheritance, strengthened by millennia of trading and social contact between highland and lowland peoples.

First was the belief that humanity originated at Lake Titicaca, and that Viracocha was the creator god. Second was the concept that, wherever they lived, a tribal group identified a particular place or feature in their landscape as the place from which they emerged. Third was a dual relationship between local people and a group of outsiders, which, whether it was portrayed as one of co-operation or conflict, defined the nature of how the groups interrelated. Finally, there was the conviction that there was a correct ordering of society and place in terms of rank and hierarchy.

Left: Lake Titicaca, with its sacred waters, came to be regarded by Andean peoples as the birthplace of the world.

CAVES, TUNNELS AND ISLANDS

The Earth, the Lower World of Hurin Pacha, lay between the worlds of Hanan Pacha (the World Above) and Uku Pacha (the World Below). Also known as Kai Pacha, it was the physical world in which humans lived, and was, theoretically speaking, flat. Completing the cycle of the universe, it was connected to the worlds above and below.

The celestial river of Mayu, the Milky Way, channelled water across the heavens, having collected it from earthly sources – a perfect representation of the endless cycle, *pachacuti*. In theory, all living things on Earth had celestial counterparts in stellar and dark cloud constellations (the spaces between the stars). Connection to the underworld was through caves, underground tunnels and springs.

MOTHER EARTH

Crucial in Andean and coastal peoples' belief was worship of mother earth, or Pacha Mama, as she was known to the Incas. To peoples so closely involved with agriculture and the harvesting of the sea for their living, and thus exposed to the periodic extremes of nature, it was natural to develop belief in an all-embracing mother goddess whose whim reflected and was responsible for their environment.

The earth goddess was a primeval deity responsible for the well-being of plants and animals. Worship of her was at least as early as the first U-shaped platform groups and sunken courts, and continues to the present day in the form of offerings of coca (*Erythroxylon coca*) leaves, *chicha* maize beer, and prayers on all major agricultural occasions. She is sometimes identified with the Virgin Mary of Christianity. In one myth, the Inca founders sacrificed and offered a llama to Pacha Mama before they entered Cuzco to take it over. One of the sister/wives, Mama Huaco, sliced open the animal's chest, extracted the lungs and inflated them with her own breath, then carried them into the city alongside Manco Capac, who carried the gold emblem of the sun god Inti.

Above: The first age in Inca creation was inevitably interpreted by author Guaman Poma de Ayala as Adam and Eve.

CAVES

These were believed to be the openings from which people emerged to inhabit the Earth. In the story of the creator god Viracocha, he created the second race of human beings from clay – the Earth. Having painted his creations with distinctive clothes and given them the different languages and customs that would distinguish them, he breathed life into them and caused them to descend into the earth and disperse. In his wandering he called them forth, to re-emerge through caves, and from lakes and hills.

The cave also features in the battle between the coastal creator god, Pachacamac, and the malevolent deity, Wakon, a classic duel between good and evil. Wakon lurked in a cave, enticed the twin son and daughter of Pachacamac and Pacha Mama and sent them to fetch water so he could seduce their mother.

Left: The massive gateway entrance to the Kalasasaya compound at Tiwanaku, which was surrounded by a moat.

Having done so and then destroyed her, it was the humble spider, servant of the Earth, who tricked Wakon in his search for the twins by laying a mountain chasm trap, into which Wakon fell and was destroyed.

SACRED LINKS

Caves were linked by tunnels running beneath the earth. Using these tunnels, the peoples created by Viracocha were thus redistributed throughout the known world. In one of the many versions of the Inca creation myth, it was held that the ancestors were born on the Island of the Sun, in Lake Titicaca. The senior ancestor, Manco Capac, led them from there, underground, to Capac Toco cave at Pacaritambo, south-west of Cuzco, from which they emerged to take over the valley.

The original inhabitants of the Cajatambo region, in highland central Peru, were the Guaris. Their patron god was a giant called Huari, who lived among the caves. Another important Guari deity was the 'night-time sun' – the sun after sunset, which it was believed passed through a hidden, underground watery passage until the next day's sunrise.

Left: The first Inca 'coat of arms' showed elements of their origin: Inti, Quilla and the cave from which the Inca ancestors emerged.

These sacred links between Mother Earth, the sky deities and the underworld were symbolized in ceremonial architecture from earliest times. U-shaped structures and sunken courts feature from the Initial Period to the Late Horizon. The inner labyrinths of temples, particularly at Chavín de Huántar, mimic cave-like mystery. Paracas and Nazca tombs were cave-like structures in which descendants could inter ancestors and re-enter to place more burials within them. They were places of symbolic rebirth through mummification, as well as of burial. The underground water channels of Cahuachi can also be regarded as links. Life-giving waters that had disappeared into the earth on their course from the mountains was tapped underground and brought to the surface for the rebirth of the crops in an endless cycle. Ritual processions through ceremonial complexes descended into the sunken court – a symbolic cave of creation

Above: Inca ancestors would have approached Cuzco across the southern mountains, including sacred Mt Ausangate (centre left).

– before being reborn to ascend the celestial heights of the platform to complete the link with the upper world.

ISLANDS

These were also significant in the mythology of creation. The Island of the Sun and the Island of the Moon in Lake Titicaca were believed to be the birthplaces of the celestial bodies, created by Viracocha, and from which they were caused to rise into the heavens. The sacred Akapana and Kalasasaya compound at Tiwanaku were surrounded by a moat, effectively making it an island, whether or not the moat was actually filled with water.

The Incas recognized the ancient sacredness of Tiwanaku not only because of the significance of the Islands of the Sun and the Moon, but also as the birthplace of an earlier race of beings – giants who preceded the Incas and were represented by the great stone statues at the site.

AGES OF MAN

The most important ancient Andean religious theme is continuity, progressing in cycles of events through time. Despite changes to the landscape, climatic change and the ebb and flow of political change, generations of Andean peoples developed beliefs in a sequence of ages that led through a series of creation efforts to their own times. The final expression of this theme was recorded as the Incas told it to Spanish chroniclers.

THE AGE OF GIANTS

The creator god was, to name him fully, Con Tici Viracocha Pachayachachic – 'creator of all things'. He rose from the deep waters of Lake Titicaca and created the first world, a world without light. There was no sun, moon or stars. Viracocha made giant models of beings in his own likeness, which he painted. He wanted to see if it would be a good thing to have a race of people who were that large. They lived in darkness and were unable to worship him.

Below: Lake Titicaca, the most sacred place in the Andean world, where Viracocha made the world and all its forms and living beings.

Viracocha ordered these giants to live without conflict and to obey and worship him. But they did not obey him, and in retribution he turned them into stone and other features of the landscape. The Incas regarded the great stone statues among the ruins of Tiwanaku as a record of this first age.

It began to rain and continued to do so for 60 days and 60 nights. A great flood known as *unu pachacuti* – 'water that overturns the land' – engulfed the land. Some giants, who had not been turned into stone, were destroyed by the waters and swallowed into the earth. Some people believed that all living things were drowned in the flood, but it seems that one man and one woman of normal size survived by hiding in a box or drum, which floated on the flood waters and came to land at Tiwanaku.

THE SUN, MOON AND STARS

Con Tici Viracocha next went to the Island of the Sun, in Lake Titicaca, near Tiwanaku. There he made the sun, moon and stars and ordered them to ascend into the heavens to give light to the world. He set them in motion to create the cycle

Above: The Incas regarded such great stone statues as the Ponce Stela at Tiwanaku to be a record of the first age of giants.

of day and night, the waxing and waning of the moon and the progression of the seasons. The moon shone more brightly than the sun, and the sun became jealous. In rage, he threw ashes into the moon's face, diminishing its glow and causing the shades of grey on its surface.

A SECOND AGE OF HUMANS

Viracocha then returned to Tiwanaku and created a second race of humans. This time he wanted his creation to be more perfect, so he created men and women of a stature similar to his own. He sculpted these beings from 'the pliable stones' of the lakeshore – meaning clay. He painted the men and women of different nations and tribes with their characteristic costumes, hairstyles and jewellery. He gave each

designated group its own language, special songs and the precious gift of agriculture in the form of seeds to sow.

Viracocha then dispersed these peoples throughout the land by causing them to descend into Mother Earth and to migrate

Below: Viracocha was represented in many stone images at Tiwanaku, usually in Staff Deity pose, recalling the ancient Chavín god.

to their 'places of origin' (*pacarinas*). They were instructed to wait there as *mitimaes* (the name given to communities forcibly resettled by the Incas) until called forth to inhabit the land. (This arrangement clearly fitted Inca notions that they were the chosen people with a right to rule others, for Viracocha seems to anticipate what would happen when the Incas began to create their empire.)

Two men, called his sons or brothers, were kept aside as his helpers. Viracocha taught them the names of the various peoples and told them to memorize their designated valleys and provinces of origin. He said, 'just as I have made them they must come out of the springs and rivers and caves and mountains'. He instructed each helper on his route, directing each to start by heading towards the sunset. Lastly, Viracocha made a sacred idol on the Island of the Sun to commemorate what had been accomplished.

CALLING FORTH THE NATIONS

The brother-son Imaymana Viracocha travelled north-west along the border of the mountains and jungles. Tocapu Viracocha went to the coast and travelled north along the ocean provinces. Con Tici

Above: The Incas recognized the Island of the Sun, in Lake Titicaca, as the birth place of the sun and moon, and built a temple there.

himself went between them, following the highlands, towards Cuzco along the River Vilcanota. As they passed through the land, they called forth the nations, telling the people to obey the orders of Con Tici – to spread across the valleys, settle the land and multiply.

A third helper (in one variation), Taguapaca, refused to follow Viracocha's commands. Viracocha ordered Imaymana and Tocapu to seize Taguapaca, bind his hands and feet and throw him into the river. Cursing and vowing to return to take vengeance, Taguapaca was carried by the river into Lake Titicaca and disappeared. Much later he reappeared and travelled to preach, saying that he was Viracocha, but people were suspicious and most ridiculed him.

The three Viracochas taught the people and performed many miracles in their travels, finally reaching the end of their journey on the north-west coast. Viracocha (or, in one version, all three) continued out to sea, walking on the water (or in a boat made from his cloak).

TALES OF HEROES

Heroes and rulers of the most ancient times are unknown because there are no written sources to name them. It is not until the Later Intermediate Period and the Late Horizon that there are accounts of legendary kings and their dynasties, and several legendary heroes who stand out among the ancient Andean cultures. Apart from obvious figures in the Inca state creation myth – Manco Capac and his brothers and sisters – there are a few founders of dynasties in pre-Inca cultures whose legends have survived because they were important in some way to Inca imperial claims to rulership and territory. They have survived in turn through the Spanish chroniclers.

The ancient Moche deities are, for the most part, unnamed except by epithets created by archaeologists – for example the Decapitator God and the bird deities depicted in painted ritual scenes. If the

Right: The Naymlap dynasty afforded noble burials filled with exquisitely crafted burial gear, such as this gold hip plate.

priests impersonating these deities were also rulers, their names are likewise unknown, even though their reality is confirmed in the rich burials of the Moche Lords of Sipán, burials with all the rich trappings of rulership and a style of dress identical to the figures in the painted scenes. Royal dynasties are again attested by the rich burials of the later Sicán Lords of the Lambayeque Valley farther north.

The story of the founding of a dynasty of kings, so clearly attested by these archaeological discoveries in the northern coastal valleys, however, emerges in the legend of Naymlap, a founder hero.

Above: This pair of Moche turquoise and gold earrings from Sipán, c.AD 400, shows warriors carrying spears and ropes and reflects the richness of Naymlap's 'noble company'.

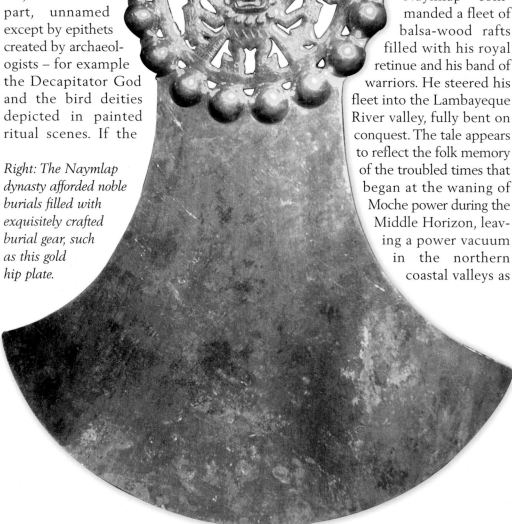

THE TALE OF NAYMLAP

Naymlap commanded a fleet of balsa-wood rafts filled with his royal retine and his band of warriors. He steered his fleet into the Lambayeque River valley, fully bent on conquest. The tale appears to reflect the folk memory of the troubled times that began at the waning of Moche power during the Middle Horizon, leaving a power vacuum in the northern coastal valleys as

Wari and Tiwanaku rulers built powerful sierra empires farther south. It seems that Naymlap, even if only one among several powerful war leaders, stepped into the breach and may be one of the first real people of ancient Andean civilization known today. The Lambayeque (or Sicán) culture that succeeded the Moche appears to have been a loose confederation of petty states in these northern coastal valleys, possibly linked through dynastic inheritance and royal descent as the sons of kings founded sister cities in the adjacent valleys.

A BRAVE AND NOBLE COMPANY

Naymlap led a 'brave and noble company' of men and women. Accompanying him were his wife, Ceterni, his harem and 40 followers. There were Pitz Zofi, Preparer of the Way; Fonga Sigde, Blower of the Conch Trumpet; Ninacola, Master of the Royal Litter and Throne; Ninagintue, the Royal Cellerer (presumably for *chicha* beer); Llapchillulli, Provider of Feather Garments; Xam Muchec, Steward of the Face-paint; Occhocalo, the Royal Cook; and Ollopcopoc, Master of the Bath.

Naymlap also brought his symbol of royal power, the greenstone idol called Yampallec, from which the Lambayeque Valley takes its name. The idol's visage, stature and figure was a double of the king himself.

NAYMLAP'S DYNASTY

With his men, Naymlap invaded the valley and built a palace at the place called Chot, which archaeologists have identified as the site of Huaca Chotuna in the Lambayeque Valley. The conquest of the local peoples was successful, and together the invaders and invaded settled down in peace. After a long life, Naymlap died and was buried in the palace. He had

Below: Detail of a gold and jade kero, *or cup, from Lambeyeque, which may show the legendary dynasty founder Naymlap.*

Left: Like the earlier Naymlap dynasty, founders of the Chimú dynasty in the Moche and other northern coastal valleys came from the south by sea in balsa boats, represented in this Chimú ceramic vessel.

arranged in secret with his priests, however, that they should tell his people that upon his death he had sprouted wings and flown away into the sky.

Naymlap was succeeded by his eldest son, Cium, and thereafter by ten other kings in his dynasty, until the last ruler, Fempellec. Cium married a local woman named Zolzoloñi. The Spanish text refers to Zolzoloñi by the word *moza*, 'commoner' or 'outsider', making it clear that she was not one of Naymlap's people or descendants. Cium and Zolzoloñi had 12 sons, each of whom married and also produced large families. As the population of the valley grew, each son left the capital and founded a new city within the valley.

A DYNASTY BETRAYED

Fempellec was the 12th ruler of the dynasty. Unlike its founder, however, he is noteworthy for having brought dishonour and disaster to the kingdom. He was insistent upon a plan to remove the stone idol of Yampallec from Chot to another city, an act of which his priests heartily disapproved. Before he could accomplish this sacrilege, however, a demon appeared to him in the form of a beautiful woman. She seduced him, and after his betrayal it began to rain heavily, an event all too rare in the region. It rained for 30 days, and then was followed by a year of drought and, inevitably, hunger, as the crops failed.

By this time the priests had tired of their scheming ruler. They seized Fempellec and tied his hands and feet; carried him to the sea, threw him in, and left him to his fate, thus ending the dynasty of Naymlap and his successors.

The legend of Naymlap is so lost in time that it is impossible to be certain whether his tale is to be associated with the founding of the Early Intermediate Period Moche, or one of its dynasties, or with the Late Intermediate Period Kingdom of Chimú, or indeed with the intervening Lambayeque (Sicán) civilization.

THE KINGDOM OF THE CHIMÚ

The Late Intermediate Period kingdom of Chimú (or Chimor) occupied the northern coastal valleys the Moche had previously occupied, filling the power vacuum apparently left by the collapse of the Moche and Lambayeque-Sicán dynasties. Chimú was centred in the Moche Valley, south of Lambayeque. Again there are stories of legendary rulers; early accounts were handed down through the generations before being recorded by the later kings of Chimú and the Incas, then passed on through Spanish chroniclers.

A NEW DYNASTY

Taycanamu was the first of a new Chimú dynasty established in the 14th century. Like so many pre-Inca rulers in the kingdoms subjugated by them, knowledge of the dynasty is obscured in legend. Taycanamu was said to have arrived at Moche on a balsa-wood raft, 'sent' from afar with the express mission of governing the peoples of the valley. Was he a late descendant of the northern dynasties? Several unnamed and little-known kings succeeded him until the conquest of the valley by the Inca prince Tupac Yupanqui in the mid-15th century. The *ciudadella* compounds at the capital, Chan Chan, appear to be the dedicated sacred compounds of the succeeding kings of Chimú.

Chimo Capac, literally 'Lord Chimú', was undoubtedly one of these kings. In the late 14th or early 15th century he invaded the Lambayeque Valley from Moche, possibly after the death of Fempellec and his contemporaries. Like Naymlap, he came by sea. He appointed a man named Pongmassa to rule the valley as the local *curaca* (official), then returned to Chan Chan. Pongmassa was succeeded by his son and grandson. During the grandson's time, the Incas invaded and subjugated Chimú. As was characteristic Inca policy, they

Above: The administrative sector of Chan Chan, capital of Chimú and South America's largest pre-Hispanic mud-brick settlement.

continued to rule the valley through its local *curaca*, five more of whom succeeded before the Spanish Conquest.

THE SUBJUGATION OF CHIMÚ

Minchançaman (or Minchancamon) was the last of the independent rulers of the Taycanamu dynasty, the sixth or seventh ruler in that line. The account of Tupac Yupanqui's invasion demonstrates the Incas' method of incorporating new kingdoms into the fabric of the empire, firmly establishing their overlordship while at the same time recognizing the integrity and power of the ruling dynasty:

'The brave Chimú [Minchançaman], his arrogance and pride now tamed, appeared before the prince [Tupac Yupanqui] with as much submission and

humility, and grovelled on the ground before him, worshipping him and repeating the same request [for pardon] as he had made through his ambassadors. The prince received him affectionately in order to relieve [his] grief ... [and] bade two of the captains raise him from the ground. After hearing him [Tupac Yupanqui] told him that all that was past was forgiven.... The Inca had not come to deprive him of his estates and authority, but to improve his idolatrous religion, his laws, and his customs.'

TALES FROM THE SOUTH

The abandonment of the ceremonial city of Tiwanaku on the southern shores of Lake Titicaca occurred at the end of the Middle Horizon. Archaeological evidence indicates that the withdrawal from use of the various monumental structures and ceremonial courts was quite abrupt, even violent. We can only speculate as to why the rulers of the city abandoned it or were overthrown. However, one tale from Inca

Below: A drawing by Guaman Poma de Ayala showing humans from the first age cultivating the crops and tilling the land.

records that may be relevant tells of the legendary rulers of two city-states in the Titicaca Basin, Cari and Zapana.

Cari sought the help of the Incas of Cuzco against his rival Zapana. The Incas, however, saw this as an opportunity (or an invitation) to invade the region and to subjugate both cities. Although the story dates from long after the civilization of Tiwanaku had collapsed, the still visible ruins were revered by the Incas. They recognized that the city was ancient and had been powerful. The ruins inspired them to use these invasions to claim descent from the ancient rulers or deities of the region. Perhaps the story is a long folk memory of the break-up of Tiwanaku, recording how rival factions within the Titicaca Basin sought the help of the Incas as the rising power in the Cuzco Valley to the north-west.

THE UNNAMED MAN

A mysterious figure features in the story of Inca beginnings – the Unnamed Man. The Incas divided their empire into four parts and referred to it as Tahuantinsuyu – land of the four quarters – which were named Chinchaysuyu, Antisuyu, Cuntisuyu and Collasuyu. The story of the Unnamed Man is the only substantial account of this division and of the appointment and naming of the *suyu* (quarter) rulers.

Above: From the Titicaca Basin, backdrop to the ancient city of Tiwanaku, the Unnamed Man appeared after the great flood.

After the waters of the great world flood receded, a powerful, but unnamed, man appeared at the ancient city of Tiwanaku in the Titicaca Basin. The Unnamed Man used his powers to designate the four quarters and to appoint rulers for each of them. To Chinchaysuyu (the north) he named Manco Capac; to Collasuyu (the south) he named Colla; to Antisuyu (the east) he named Tocay; to Cuntisuyu (the west) he named Pinahua. He commanded each king to conquer his allotted quarter and to govern his people.

The brief story is recounted in Garcilaso de la Vega's *Commentarios Reales de los Incas*. The dearth of further explanation is curious, given Inca emphasis on their origins at Lake Titicaca in one version of the official state creation myth. Recognizing Tiwanaku as an ancient seat of power, they wished to bolster their claimed right to rule. Tiwanaku was, in fact, much closer to the actual centre of the empire than was Cuzco.

The rich lands of the Lupaqa Kingdoms – the late inheritors of Tiwanaku power – were important acquisitions to the Inca, as were the vast llama lands of the Altiplano.

EL DORADO AND CHIBCHA HEROES

Although the Chibcha area of present-day Colombia is not technically in the Andean Area, no book on ancient Andean mythology would seem complete without a description of the legend of El Dorado.

THE GILDED MAN

El Dorado, literally the 'Gilded Man' in Spanish, was the legendary king of the chiefdom of the Chibcha, or Muisca, of the far northern Andes in Colombia. El Dorado was a person, a city, an entire kingdom and, in time, a myth. In their lust for gold, once tales of untold wealth from that quarter had reached their ears, the Spaniards generally associated the legend with the entire region of

Below: The myth of El Dorado was represented in a multi-necklace- and earring-wearing man from the Calima culture.

central Colombia. In reality, the quest for gold and riches beyond belief turned out to be a chimera: El Dorado was always just one more range of mountains away, but was never found.

The most reliable sources of the legend focus on the Chibcha/Muisca and their chiefdom around Lake Guatavita in central Colombia, north of Bogotá. Gold was extremely important to all the chiefdoms of the far northern Andes, and several distinctive gold-working styles developed throughout the region from the first century BC/AD; the Muisca style itself dates from the 8th century AD. The Spaniards learned the story of the Gilded Man from many sources, including the Chibcha, who had actually witnessed the ceremony before the Spaniards arrived. Every conquistador and chronicler of this northern area makes mention of the Gilded Man, but the most complete account is that of the mid-17th-century chronicler Rodríguez Freyle, who was told the legend by his friend Don Juan, the nephew of the last independent lord of Guatavita.

THE ANOINTING OF A KING

The ritual that gave rise to the legend was performed at the inauguration of a new king. The heir to the throne spent the days before the ceremony secluded in a cave. During this time, he was required to abstain from sexual relations with women and was forbidden to eat chilli peppers or salt. On the appointed day, he made his first official journey to Lake Guatavita, there to make offerings to the gods. At the lakeside, a raft of rushes was made and bedecked with precious decorations and treasures. Four lighted braziers were placed on the raft, in which *moque* incense and other resins were burned. Braziers of incense were also lit along the

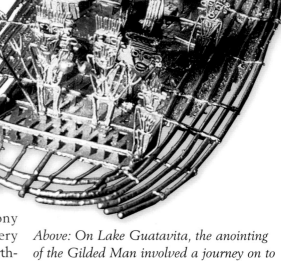

Above: On Lake Guatavita, the anointing of the Gilded Man involved a journey on to the lake and the deposition of golden gifts.

shoreline, and such a quantity of smoke was produced by them that the light of the sun was said to be obscured.

The king-to-be was stripped naked and his body smeared with a sticky clay or resin. Over this he was covered with glittering gold dust, shown being blown from a tube in an engraving of 1599. He then boarded the raft, accompanied by four principal subject chiefs, all of whom were richly attired in 'plumes, crowns, bracelets, pendants, and ear rings all of gold', but also otherwise naked. The king remained motionless on the raft and at his feet was placed a great heap of gold and precious stones (called 'emeralds' by Freyle).

The raft was pushed off across the lake, whereupon musicians on shore struck up a fanfare of trumpets, flutes and other instruments, and the assembled crowd began to sing loudly. When the raft reached the centre of the lake, a banner

was raised as a signal for silence. The gilded king then made his offering to the gods: all of the treasures on the raft were thrown into the lake, one by one, by the king and his attendants. Then the flag was lowered again, and the raft paddled towards shore to the accompaniment of loud music and singing, and wild dancing.

Upon reaching the shore, the new king was accepted as the lord and master of the realm.

CHIBCHA LEGENDS

A few Chibcha heroes are known. Bochica was their legendary founder hero. He arrived among them from the east, travelling as a bearded sage, and taught them civilization, moral laws and the craft

Below: Guatavita, the 'El Dorado' lake in Colombia where Chibcha chiefs dived covered in clay and powdered gold.

of metalworking. Not all accepted his teaching, however. A woman named Chie challenged him by urging the Chibcha to ignore him and make merry, whereupon Bochica transformed her into an owl.

Above: Skilled gold-workers from northern cultures in Colombia produced items such as this embossed breastplate with ear disks.

Even so, she helped the god Chibchacum (patron of metalworkers and merchants) to flood the Earth. Bochica appeared as a rainbow, then as the sun. He sent his rays to evaporate the waters, and created a channel by striking the rocks with his golden staff for the water to drain into the sea. He was worshipped as the sun god Zue, and Chie became the moon goddess.

A parallel tale concerns an old bearded man called Nemterequeteba, who came to the Muisca from a distant land. He, too, taught the Chibcha the art of weaving and civilized behaviour. His rival was Huitaca, goddess of evil and patroness of misbehaviour and drunkenness. She challenged Nemterequeteba and in one version of the legend she was transformed into the moon by him. She is therefore sometimes confused with the Muisca moon goddess Chie.

The obscurity of these tales might reflect troubles on the distant northern borders of the Inca or earlier kingdoms. Chie/Huitaca, clearly a local deity, resented the appearance of an outsider from afar, who came essentially in a guise similar to the wandering creator god Viracocha.

EMPIRE OF THE SUN

Manco Capac was the legendary first Inca ruler and founder of the Inca dynasty Hurin Cuzco. He was the principal character in Inca mythology surrounding the origins of the state and Inca power.

THE STATE CREATION MYTH

Various permutations of the Inca state creation myth prevailed simultaneously, a fact that caused the Spanish chroniclers considerable consternation. The most prominent version described how four brothers and four sisters came forth from the central one of three 'windows', or caves, in the mountain called Tambo Toco ('window mountain'). These were 'the ancestors', led by the eldest brother, Manco Capac (originally Ayar Manco), who, with his brothers (Ayar Auca, Ayar Cachi and Ayar Uchu) and sisters (Mama Ocllo, Mama Huaco, Mama Ipacura/Cura and Mama Raua), led the people of Tambo Toco in search of a new land to settle, where a capital city could be built.

Below: The endurance of Inca culture is exemplified by this characteristic Inca trapezoidal doorway in Cuzco, still in use.

Above: Manco Capac, legendary founder of the Inca dynasty and 'son of the sun'.

After much wandering they came to a hill overlooking the Cuzco Valley. Miraculous signs informed them that they should settle there, so they came down from the mountain, overcame local resistance and took possession of the land.

EMERGENCE FROM CAPAC TOCO

The standard version comes from Sarmiento de Gamboa, in his *Historia de los Incas* (1572), an early source that relied heavily on interviews with keepers of the Inca state records, the *quipucamayoqs*.

Pacaritambo, overlooking which was Tambo Toco, was the 'house of dawn', the 'place of origin'. According to the chroniclers it was six leagues (about 33km/20 miles) south of Cuzco; in fact, it is closer to 26km (16 miles). In the beginning, the mountain there, Tambo Toco, had three windows, the central one of which was called Capac Toco – 'rich window'. From this window emerged the four ancestral couples, the brother/sister–husband/wife pairs: Capac with Ocllo, Auca with Huaco, Cachi with Ipacura/ Cura, and Uchu with Raua. From the flanking windows, Maras Toco and Sutic Toco, came

the peoples called the Maras and the Tambos, both Inca allies. A divine link was immediately established in the promotion of the myth when it was claimed that the ancestors and allies were called out of the caves by Con Tici Viracocha.

Ayar Manco declared that he would lead his brothers and sisters, and the allies, in search of a fertile land, where the local inhabitants would be conquered. He promised to make the allies rich. Before setting out, the allies were formed into ten *ayllus* (lineage groups) – the origin of the ten *ayllus* of Cuzco commoners. The ten royal *ayllus* (called *panacas*) were the descendants of the first ten Inca emperors.

THE JOURNEY BEGINS

Ayar Manco led his followers north, towards the Cuzco Valley. He carried a golden bar, brought from Tambo Toco. With this he tested the ground for fertility by thrusting it periodically into the soil.

Progress was slow and there were several stops. At the first stop Ayar Manco and Mama Ocllo conceived a child. At the second stop a boy was born, whom they named Sinchi Roca. They stopped a third time at a place called Palluta, where they lived for several years; but eventually the

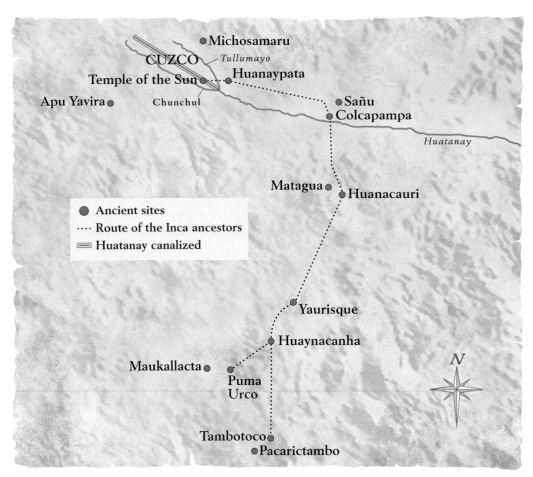

Ancient sites
Route of the Inca ancestors
Huatanay canalized

land proved unfertile, so they moved on to a place called Haysquisrro. Here the company began to break up.

BREAKING UP OF THE COMPANY

Ayar Cachi was unruly and sometimes cruel. He always caused trouble with the local inhabitants through his tricks and rowdiness wherever the ancestors passed through or stopped. He was a powerful slinger, and could hurl stones so hard that he could split open mountains, causing dust and rocks to fly up and obscure the sun. The other ancestors began to consider him a liability, so they formed a plan to dispense with him. Manco told Cachi that several important objects that should have accompanied the golden rod had been left in Pacaritambo: a golden cup (*topacusi*), a miniature llama figurine (*napa*) and some seeds. Ayar Cachi at first refused to return to Capac Toco, but agreed to do so when his elder sister, Mama Huaco, herself forceful in character, chided him and accused him of laziness and cowardice.

Below: A fanciful Spanish genealogy of Inca emperors, from Manco Capac onward.

Cachi journeyed back to Capac Toco with a Tambo companion called Tambochacay ('the Tambo entrance-bearer'). He was unaware, however, that Manco and the others had convinced Tambochacay to get rid of him. When Ayar Cachi entered the cave to retrieve the forgotten items, Tambochacay quickly

Above: After their underground migration from Lake Titicaca and emergence from a cave, the Inca ancestor pairs went to Cuzco.

sealed off the entrance, trapping Cachi inside forever. The site, later known as Mauqallaqta ('ancient town'), became an important Inca sacred *huaca*.

The ancestors' next stop was Quirirmanta, at the foot of a mountain called Huanacauri. They climbed the mountain, and from the top saw the Cuzco Valley for the first time. From the summit, Manco threw the golden rod into the valley to test the soil. To the ancestors' amazement the rod disappeared into the Earth and a rainbow appeared over the valley. They took these signs to mean that this should be their homeland.

Before they could descend the mountain, Ayar Uchu sprouted wings and flew up to the sun. The sun told him that, thenceforth, Ayar Manco should be called Manco Capac, the 'supreme rich one', and that they should go to Cuzco, where the ruler, Alcavicça, would welcome them. Uchu returned to his brothers and sisters, told them this news, and was transformed into stone, becoming a second *huaca*.

85

Inca Cuzco (the plaza called Huanay-pata), the remaining brother-ancestor, Ayar Auca, was turned into a stone pillar, which, like Mauqallaqta and Uchu, became a sacred *huaca*.

This left Manco Capac, his sisters and his son Sinchi Roca, a convenient outcome, which was in keeping with later Inca imperial practice of sister/wives, and a chosen descendant to the rulership. They began the building of Cuzco.

INCA AMBITIONS

This 'standard' version contains all the necessary elements of Inca legend, including in mythical form the wandering, conquering, alliances and divine intervention needed to telescope what must have been the folk memory of their long and complex history.

Left: A fanciful 18th-century Spanish colonial depiction of an Inca prince sporting a sun pendant, indicating his imperial status.

Below: Regarded as the 'sons of the sun', Inca emperors were carried about in stately fashion on a litter, shown here on a wooden kero *cup.*

THE FINAL ROAD TO CUZCO

However, the remaining ancestors did not proceed straight to Cuzco. They stopped first at nearby Matao, where they stayed for two years, and where another strange event occurred. Mama Huaco, an expert slinger, hurled a stone at a man in Matao and killed him. She split open his chest, removed his heart and lungs and blew into the lungs to inflate them. The watching people of the town fled in terror.

Finally, Manco Capac led the ancestors to Cuzco. They met Alcavicça and declared that they had been sent by their father, the sun, which convinced Alcavicça to allow them to take over. In return the ancestors 'domesticated' the inhabitants of the valley by teaching them to plant maize. (In one version it was Manco Capac who planted the first field; in another it was Mama Huaco.) At the place that would become the centre of

The Incas were ambitious, however. They felt a need to link their personal creation to world creation, and thus legitimize their right to rule through divine sanction. They vigorously promoted their own political agenda, and were particularly keen to establish their origins as special and to convince others that *their* place of origin was universal – that is, the same as that of the Incas. The 17th-century Jesuit priest Bernabé Cobo describes this official state line as 'caused by the ambition of the Incas. They were the first to worship [at] the cave of Pacaritambo as the [place of the] beginning of their lineage. They claimed that all people came from there, and that for this reason all people were their vassals and obliged to serve them'.

VARIATIONS ON A THEME

In other variations of the story, the Incas were more devious – they rewrote and reshaped their story to justify their actions and to incorporate long-held beliefs of the peoples they subjugated. Thus, in one version the ancestors deliberately tricked the inhabitants of the Cuzco Valley into believing them to be the descendants of the sun, not just his ambassadors. Manco Capac made, or had made, two golden discs – one for his front, one for his back. He climbed Mt Huanacauri before dawn so that at sunrise he appeared to be a golden, god-like being. The populace of Cuzco was so awed that he had no trouble in assuming rulership.

Another version, given by four elderly *quipucamayoqs*, contains an undercurrent of the resentment that must have been harboured by local inhabitants at the outsiders' invasion. The story suggests that the whole fabric of Inca rule was illegitimate.

In this variation, Manco Capac was the son of a local *curaca* in Pacaritambo, whose mother had died giving birth to him. His father gave him the nickname 'son of the sun', but also died, when Manco Capac was 10 or 12, never having

Above: The large oval eyes, feline grin, snake, trophy head and other symbols of this sheet-gold Inca sun disk seem to be a composite of sacred ancient Andean iconography.

explained that it was just a nickname. What is more, the commoners of the town were convinced that Manco was actually the son of the sun, and the two old priests of his father's household gods encouraged this belief. As Manco Capac reached early manhood, the priests promoted Manco's conviction, telling him that it gave him the right to rule. Filled with this idea, he set off for Cuzco with several relatives and the priests, taking his

father's idol, Huanacauri. He arrived on Mt Huanacauri at dawn, bedecked in gold, thus dazzling the people and convincing them of his divine descent Yet another version of the state origin myth associates the ancestors with the Island of the Sun in Lake Titicaca, from which Manco Capac led them underground to Pacaritambo. This was a deception meant to justify Inca conquest. Being born on the Island of the Sun made Manco Capac 'son of the sun'. Local myth described a great deluge that destroyed the previous world and claimed that the sun of the present world first shone on the island. He placed his son and daughter on the island to teach the locals how to live civilized lives. The Incas believed that these were Manco Capac and Mama Ocllo, and that the creator, Viracocha, bestowed a special headdress and stone battle-axe upon Manco Capac, prophesying that the Incas would become great lords and conquer many other nations.

Below: In a 20th-century revival of the Inti Raymi (June/winter solstice festival) women are dressed to represent acllas *virgins.*

ISLANDS OF THE SUN AND MOON

The Island of the Sun and the Island of the Moon were sacred places in the southern half of Lake Titicaca, just offshore north of the Copacabana Peninsula. Sitting almost at the centre of the lake, the Island of the Sun was a dramatic location from which to observe the passage of the sun across the high, clear mountain sky. The Incas believed that the islands were the birthplaces of the sun and the moon, or that the sun, moon and stars were created and set in motion from the Island of the Sun by the god Con Tici Viracocha Pachayachachic – 'creator of all things'.

A MOST SACRED PLACE

The Incas identified and named the Island of the Sun and built a shrine there dedicated to Viracocha. The shrine was the focus of an annual pilgrimage by the Inca emperor and nobility. Alongside the sacred Coricancha in Cuzco, and the much more ancient shrine and oracle to Pachacamac in the central coastal city of the same name, this shrine was one of the most sacred sites in the Inca realm until

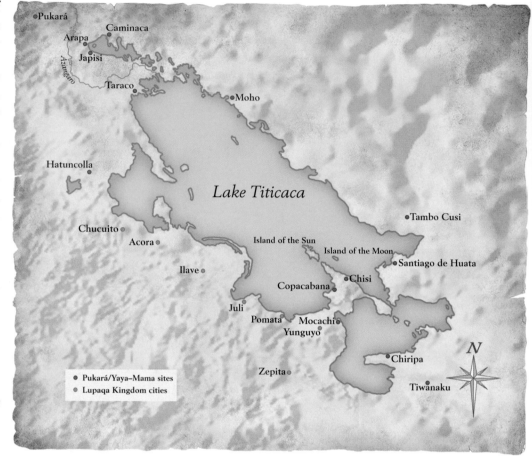

Above: This map shows Lake Titicaca, with the sacred Islands of the Sun and Moon, and ancient sites of religious importance.

Below: The sacred Island of the Sun, Lake Titicaca, rising steeply from the lake, where Viracocha created the sun and the moon.

sacked by the Spaniards in their lust for gold. A sacred stone – the Rock of the Sun, a partially modified natural boulder – set up in an open space, and from which the sun was believed to have risen, still stands on the island overlooking the lake.

In one version of the Inca state creation story Manco Capac and his sister/wife Mama Ocllo (and in some variations their siblings as well) were associated with the Island of the Sun in a deception meant to justify Inca conquest of the local peoples. They were said to have led their brothers and sisters from the Island of the Sun, either through the earth or overland to the caves at Pacaritambo.

A PRE-INCA CULT

When the Inca emperor Pachacuti subjugated the Titicaca Basin in the mid-15th century, part of his task was made easier by entering into alliances with some of

Above: The Incas revered the site of Tiwanaku on the southern lakeshore. They built temples to Viracocha and Inti on the Island of the Sun.

the city-states there, such as the Lupaca. The Incas no doubt played on local rivalries to conquer those who resisted their incursions. Pachacuti soon realized the ancient importance of the lake and islands in local religious belief, and with characteristic Inca policy, recognized and honoured the local ruins still visible at Tiwanaku on the southern lakeshore.

Hard evidence of the pre-Inca sacredness of both islands is given by archaeological finds. Hammered sheet-gold and silver objects in the forms of cut-out llamas and the image of Tiwanaku's principal deity – the god with large round eyes and a rounded square face depicted on the Gateway of the Sun, so-called for the sun-like rays surrounding the god's face – have been found on both islands and on the mainland at Tiwanaku itself. A gold disc depicting the god, along with a gold cup and ceramic vessels, were found in the lake off Koa Island, just off the north end of the Island of the Sun. The llama features frequently in Tiwanaku and later sacrificial ritual, and clearly these objects were sacred offerings to the sun by priests or pilgrims.

AN INCA PILGRIMAGE SITE

It was Pachacuti, the great builder, who began the Inca temple and shrine on the Island of the Sun. According to Inca records the temple was administered by 2,000 cult retainers. The temple complex included a *tambo* (a way-station to accommodate pilgrims) and an *acllahuasi* (a 'house of the chosen women' known as *acllas* – hand-picked Inca girls trained to serve the cult of Inti, the sun god, who was ultimately regarded as the Inca emperor himself). In addition to the *tambo* and *acllahuasi*, storehouses were built near Copacabana to provide provisions, clothes and other supplies to the temple attendants and pilgrims.

It seems likely that the Incas adopted a much older cult of the sun established by the people of Tiwanaku, or earlier peoples, on the island. The association of the island as the birthplace of the Inca ancestors would certainly have been an advantageous link in Inca efforts to justify their belief in the right to rule others. One Spanish chronicler, the Augustinian Alonso Ramos Gavilán, claims that the local inhabitants had sent a priest to Cuzco to seek patronage from Pachacuti.

Father Bernabé Cobo devotes an entire chapter of his book on Inca religion to 'the famous temple of Copacabana'. He calls the two islands Titicaca (Sun) and Coata (Moon) and says that there were in fact 'two magnificent temples', one on each island. It is Cobo who claims that the islands were regarded as sacred before the Incas arrived in the region and declares that 'they took charge of enhancing the shrine'. Cobo describes how Tupac Yupanqui, Pachacuti's successor, undertook to enhance the shrine, first by fasting there for several days to show his devotion, and then by establishing an annual pilgrimage to the temple. To reach the Rock of the Sun, pilgrims were obliged to undergo a long ritual route including many stops for observances and offerings, both at mainland *huacas* and on the island.

Below: The extensive ruins of an acllahuasi *on the Island of the Moon bear witness to the importance of these sites of annual pilgrimage.*

CHAPTER FIVE

LEAVING THIS EARTH

The Incas regarded life and death as two of many stages in the cycle of being in which all living things took part. From birth through life and into death, there was a rhythm and sense of renewal. In a sense, in Andean belief one never 'left' the earth, for it was from the earth that people came (as described in the creation myth, when Viracocha created humans from clay, and also when they emerged from the earth into which he had dispersed them) and to it that they returned, becoming part of it at burial or remaining on it as a mummy preserved for ritual occasions.

Death did not always occur naturally, of course, and there is wide evidence of ritual sacrifice in an endless attempt to placate the gods. Once dead, rich and powerful ancient Andeans could expect an elite burial with all the trappings, possibly including mummification. Their bodies might be stored in family *chullpas* (burial towers) or buried.

The Lower World (the earth), or Hurin Pacha, was intimately linked to the World Above (Honan Pacha) and the World Below (Uku Pacha), the worlds of the gods, supernatural beings and spirits. Trained individuals, the shamans, could leave Hurin Pacha temporarily through the use of hallucinogenic drugs. They could travel in their altered mental state to converse with and seek help from the gods on behalf of individuals and the nation in general. In order to do so they could also transform into another being, for example a jaguar or an owl, taking on that being's perceived supernatural powers.

Left: Inca agricultural terracing on the steeply rising slopes above Bahia Kona on the Island of the Sun, in Lake Titicaca.

THE CYCLE OF LIFE AND DEATH

Andean belief held that the cycle of being for all living things was a procession through states of being. It began as a general vegetative state, passed through a tender, juicy young state (babies, young shoots) into a progressively drier, firmer more resistant state (adulthood, mature plant), then became a desiccated, preserved state (mummies, dried and stored crops). But this was not the end. When a person died, his or her desiccated remains were like dried pods from which seeds dropped to begin the cycle anew, as their spirit proceeded to its final resting place.

Such basic concepts seem logical in societies that were ultimately reliant on agricultural and pastoral ways of life. Birth, growth and seeding were metaphors taken from the plant world; stages of life were like those observed so closely while tending herds of llamas. The origin of each new generation from the seeds of the last was essentially an exchange of the old for the new.

Below: This Moche painted ceramic piece depicting young maize cobs on the stalk reminded the Andeans of birth and growth.

A CARING SOCIETY

During life on earth, the individual was bound into a web of mutual caring. Adults cared for babies and children just as the young cared for the aged. Each individual had their personal role in society and exchanged produce and commodities, depending on their occupation. Shamans cared for the people, while priests, who looked after the welfare of the state and were intermediaries to the gods, were supported by the people and made offerings and sacrifices to the gods on their behalf. Finally, rulers governed and redistributed the wealth of society according to each person's needs within fixed, accepted roles and stations. On a larger scale, different regions were engaged in exchange networks, both socially and for trade. Such networks of exchange were mimicked by the belief that death represented an exchange of old for new.

The Inca sources from which the Spaniards recorded these beliefs must be the culmination of beliefs from the earliest agriculturalists, refined and elaborated through millennia.

METAPHORICAL IMAGES

The cult of the founding ancestors reflects these themes. The Quechua word *mallqui* (tree) can be glossed as 'ancestor'. The three caves or windows at Tambo Toco were depicted with a tree. From the middle window, Capac Toco, came Manco Capac and the other Inca

Above: Ancient Andeans were reminded of the cycle of life by objects around them, such as this effigy bottle representing old age.

brother/sister–husband/wife ancestors. In it was a golden tree whose branches and roots connected it to the left-hand window, Maras Toco, occupied by Manco Capac's paternal ancestors. Next to the golden tree was a silver tree, connected to the right-hand window, Sutic Toco, occupied by his maternal ancestors.

Above: Ancient Andeans learned to maximize crop production through the use of natural fertilizer, such as guano from off-shore islands.

The spirits of the deceased were regarded as dangerous, and it was necessary to help them reach the end of their journey, lest they wander among the living, causing violence, sickness and accidents. To reach the Island of Guano, the *anima* was carried by sea lions. To reach Upaymarca, the spirit had to cross a broad river on a narrow bridge made of human hair, known as Achachaca (Bridge of Hairs). In one variation of the cycle, the spirit must encounter a pack of black dogs. Thus, the link is maintained between 'living' and 'dead'.

Another metaphorical depiction of regeneration and reproduction showed the *mallqui* next to the *collca*, the storehouse in which the year's harvest was kept.

Reflecting an animal metaphor, the rotting of the dead body was conceived as a process that lasted a year after the living body ceased to breathe, during which time the bodily fluids and flesh became desiccated. As this happened, the spirit of the individual emerged, just as a living seed escapes from a dried plant pod, to go to its rest.

PACARINA: RETURN TO ORIGINS

The concept of *pacarina* incorporates rebirth or regeneration. *Pacarina* was the place of origin, the place from which one's ancestors (one's tribe, nation or *ayllu* kinship group) emerged. It could be a tree, rock, cave, spring or lake, and it was a magical shelter from the ravages of the world. Andean tradition held that, after death, the spirit returned to its *pacarina* – the essence of being finally returning to its birthplace.

THE DYING PROCESS: A JOURNEY

Ancient Andeans thought of death as a gradual process, one that continued beyond the time when the body actually ceased functioning on earth, and during which the dead continued to inhabit the living world. Temporary states of being during life were regarded as near-death conditions, such as deep sleep, fainting, drunkenness and drug-induced states.

The journey ultimately began at birth. However, with the cessation of breathing and earth-life functions, the body began its death journey towards fulfilling its purpose of reunion with its ancestors and regeneration. The human spirit was the 'vital force' (Quechua *upani* or *camaquen*; Aymara *amaya* or *ch'iwu*; and in Latin/Spanish translation *alma* and *anima*).

Different sources name the spirit's final destination. Inhabitants of Collasuyu and Cuntisuyu called it Puquina Pampa and Coropuna. Cajatsmbo documents name Uma Pacha, and documents of the Lima region name Upaymarca. Coastal peoples called the final resting place the Island of Guano. More generally, the final resting place was perceived to be a land of farms, where the dead sowed their seeds. The spirit continues to tend the fields and crops, and to experience thirst and hunger as the body does on Earth, and is fed by the living with offerings of food and drink.

Right: This Moche stirrup-spouted vessel is a portrait of a living, healthy, laughing man, enjoying life to the full.

BURIAL PRACTICES

Burials of the earliest periods are rare. Few are known from the Preceramic Period, suggesting that bodies were exposed to the elements or otherwise unceremoniously disposed of. Those burials that have been found within Preceramic cave sites were mostly in a flexed position, often on one side. Food, stone tools, beds and pigment fragments were the usual grave goods. As belief in an afterlife or life cycle developed, more care was taken of the deceased, leading to the elaborate preparation and burying of bodies.

Like Paracas, the long-lived pilgrimage and oracle site of Pachacamac was a prime burial place for both rich and poor. The desire was obviously to be buried at the sacred site, and Pachacamac served a large region for more than a millennium.

BODY PRESERVATION
The Chinchorros culture of northernmost Chile provides some of the earliest mixes of ordinary and distinguished burials. Between about 8,000 and 3,600 years

Below: Inca burials were accompanied by ceremonial drinking of chicha *beer from* kero *cups to help the deceased into the next life.*

ago, most bodies were buried without special treatment. On about 250 bodies, however, a tradition of deliberate preservation is evident: bodies were de-fleshed and disarticulated, then reassembled and buried inside cane or wooden shafts. About 6,000 years ago, at La Paloma on the central Peruvian coast, corpses were salted to arrest deterioration before being placed in burial pits. These two cultures introduced the long-held practice of preservation of at least chosen individuals, and the belief that the body must be intact in order to enter the afterlife.

Burials in the late Preceramic and Initial Period onward, whether especially elaborate or not, were commonly in the shape of some type of crypt. At Preceramic Kotosh, for example, stone-built chambers were used for ritual and then as burial crypts.

SUBTERRANEAN CHAMBERS
The Early Horizon necropolis on the Paracas Peninsula has many more burials than would have been needed by the nearby surrounding settlements. It can, therefore, be concluded that it was a dedicated cemetery for communities within a large region stretching inland. The burial chambers are intermixed and show obvious social differentiation, indicated by the sizes of the burial bundles, the sizes of chambers, and the grave goods that accompanied the bodies on their final journey.

The burial chambers were large, subterranean, bottle-shaped tombs. They often contained multiple burials, indicating that they were reopened repeatedly through generations. One tomb contained 37 burial bundles. The bundles were piled on top of each other, and in some cases the largest bundle, of the most important person, was placed in the centre of the chambers and surrounded by 'his people'.

The nature of Paracas burial shows the early development of kin-group association in ancient Andean civilization. In life, kin-groups worked together within agreed

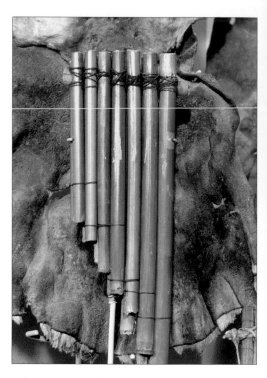

Above: Mummification techniques, together with the extreme desiccation of the Atacama Desert, preserved both human bodies and other organic matter, such as these reed pipes.

reciprocal obligations; in death, the kin-groups were buried together in their group associations over generations.

BURIAL BUNDLES
All bundles were elaborately wrapped in layers of textiles. Commoner bodies were wrapped in plain and fewer layers of cotton textiles and accompanied by plain ceramics and perhaps a few 'special' pieces. The richest burials were wrapped in much more elaborate textiles and accompanied by the richest ceramics, metalwork and exotic products from afar. Low mounds inland from the cemetery were apparently stages for the preparation of the bodies into mummy bundles.

The association of burial and rich textiles established in the Paracas and succeeding Nazca cultures was an association that continued right through to Inca society. The importance of textiles is attested by industries that produced

Above: The dry Nazca desert preserves the remains of thousands of burials, but, when exposed, the elements soon destroyed any textiles and artefacts that were not looted.

cloth exclusively for burial wrappings – which was a substantial demand on the state economy and human labour.

SUPPLIES FOR THE JOURNEY

Burial rites among most Andean peoples included gifts of clothing, food and *chicha* beer for their journey in the cycle of being.

Middle Horizon Wari tombs were often equipped with a hole in the top or side of the crypt, plus a channel to facilitate offerings of food and drink long after the individual had been laid to rest. Such feeding maintained the vital link between a people and their deceased ancestors. In Inca society, mummies were brought out on ceremonial occasions and offered food and drink.

SPECIAL PRACTICES

Burial in the Middle Horizon, Late Intermediate Period and Late Horizon was commonly in a subterranean chamber

in a seated position. Burials were often in shaft-like chambers, with later burials placed on top of earlier ones, maintaining the tradition of reopening kin-group mausoleums. Besides crypts and subterranean chambers of various sorts, several special types of burials have been discovered. For example, elongated hall-like rooms around the patios of Wari dwellings sometimes had human burials beneath their plastered floors, sometimes with small caches of valuables. The Akapana temple at Tiwanaku included ritual eating and burial, the primary burial being a man seated holding a puma effigy incense burner. In the Late Intermediate Period in the Titicaca Basin seated, subterranean chamber burials endured, but more important individuals developed the practice of burial in raised towers called *chullpas*.

One special Inca ritual practice was deliberate exposure to lightning, although it was recognized as potentially fatal.

Right: Inca funerary rites as depicted by Guaman Poma de Ayala c.1613. Note the mummified body in a chullpa *burial tower.*

A *qhaqha* (person or animals killed by lightning) was buried at the place where they were killed.

As the body was taken to its burial place, the Incas would make a mourning sound for the dead like the cooing of a dove. It was invented upon the death of the founder ancestor Ayar Uchu, according to the state creation myth.

ELITE BURIALS

Archaeological evidence from elite burials is abundant. Unfortunately, though, many rich tombs have long since been looted by treasure seekers.

ELITE INCA BURIALS

Father Bernabé Cobo, in his 17th-century *Historia del Nuevo Mundo*, describes Inca burial customs as he observed them. He declares that there was greater concern for one's place of burial than for one's dwelling when alive. Although graves and rituals varied, each province having their own practices, it was common for the elite dead to be buried lavishly. The body was dressed in all its finery – the deceased's best clothing and jewellry. Depending on the person being buried, the body would be accompanied by weapons or a person's tools of trade. Food and drink were placed on top of the dead body.

Important local men were often buried with servants and favourite wives, who would be ritually strangled before being placed in the grave, or made drunk before being buried alive with the corpse. The funeral was conducted by relatives and friends, who escorted the body to a

cemetery with mourning and chanting, dancing and heavy drinking. The ceremony lasted for a longer or shorter time according to rank. Chants recalled the most memorable deeds of the dead person, told where he or she had lived, and good deeds done by the deceased to or for the chanter.

Extremely important, legendary Inca individuals were often not 'buried' but recognized as special sacred *huacas*.

Left: Elite members of society were wrapped in numerous rich textile mantles and other garments.

Above: The Late Intermediate Period and Late Horizon Colla of the Titicaca Basin buried generations of mummified bodies in chullpas – as at the Sillustani necropolis.

According to legend, Manco Capac was turned into stone when he died. The stone was located by the Polo de Ondegardo, a Spanish magistrate, in 1559 in Membilla, now a suburb of Cuzco. A *quipu* found in an Inca burial mound indicated that the individual was an important local leader or governor.

ELITE BURIAL PARACAS STYLE

Elaborate burial accompanied by rich grave goods began in the Early Horizon Paracas culture of the southern Peruvian coast. The status of the burials in the Cavernas Paracas cemetery is revealed by the number and sumptuousness of the accompanying burial goods, since the most important individuals were sent on their journey into the afterlife with splendid riches. Less wealthy individuals were buried in plain bundles, and some bundles contained more than one body.

Right: The elite were dressed in exotic feather headgear and bone, shell and sheet-gold jewellery, preserved by the desiccating desert conditions and careful tomb burial.

Some desiccated mummy bundles were 2m (6½ft) high. Offerings included gold, feathers, animal skins and imported goods, such as shells from distant shores. Paracas bodies were tightly flexed and held together with cords. Their skulls sometimes show trepanation: pieces of skull drilled and removed by incision with an instrument or by scraping.

PREPARING A MUMMY BUNDLE

Each elite Paracas mummy bundle is unique, but its preparation and basic configuration followed important shared 'rules' or procedures.

One representative bundle was 1.7m (5½ft) high and 1.4m (4½ft) across the base. The entire bundle comprises no fewer than 25 plain cotton wraps and 44 richly decorated wraps. The body was placed on a deerskin within a large basket. Offerings of maize, yuca tuber and peanuts, and of unspun llama fibre, a *Spondylus* shell from the distant northern coast, a cloth pouch probably containing body paint, and a human skull were grouped around the body.

This assemblage was wrapped within multiple layers of cloth. Most of the pieces were wound around the body, rather than 'dressing' it. First, there are 15 embroidered garment sets, many of them unfinished, indicating that they were burial 'gifts' prepared specifically for entombment. Their decorations include common symbolic images and themes: felines, serpents, sea creatures, birds and supernatural beings.

Around these, and including the basket, were several layers of plain cotton cloth, some pieces up to 10m (33ft) long. This made the person 'larger than life' and thus emphasized their importance, as it would have been emphasized in life by the wearing of layers of loincloths,

skirts, tunics, shoulder mantles, ponchos, headbands and turban-like headgear. These outer bundles enclosed two staffs, a third staff with a feather top and an animal skeleton; six shoulder mantles; a leather cape; a bright yellow, tropical, Amazonian bird-feather tunic; and a headband. Finally, the entire mummy bundle was encased in a huge plain cloth sewn up with long stitches. It is estimated that the manufacture of the textiles and the preparation of such a bundle required anything from 5,000 to 29,000 hours.

Such elaborate ritual burial practices continued in the succeeding Nazca culture in the same region.

COLLA *CHULLPAS*

Special burials were accorded to important individuals in the Late Intermediate Period and Late Horizon Colla of the Titicaca Basin in unique *chullpa* tower stone burial chambers among the Collas people – as at the Sillustani necropolis. *Chullpas* are fitted stone volcanic masonry structures of one to three storeys, round or square in base plan. They were erected near towns or in separated groups, functioning as family mausoleums. Most *chullpas* contained generations of burials, with bodies wrapped in rich textiles, and they continued to be built into Inca times.

The richest elite burials ever found in the Americas were discovered in the Lambayeque Valley, where the Moche flourished in the Early Intermediate Period and early Middle Horizon, followed by the Lambayeque-Sicán culture of the later Middle Horizon and Early Intermediate Period. Neither used mummification.

ELITE BURIAL, MOCHE STYLE

The rich, unlooted tombs of the Moche Lords of Sipán were discovered by Walter Alva and Susana Meneses in the 1980s. The Sipán tombs reveal the riches and the exquisite craftsmanship of Moche metallurgy and ceramics. Yet Sipán was neither the capital nor the main focus of much Moche power during *c.*AD100–800. It is hard to imagine what riches have been lost that must have come from looted tombs, or that lie as yet undiscovered in unfound Moche tombs.

At Sipán, altogether twelve tombs were found in six levels of generations of burial. In the lowest level was the 'Old

Below: Ritual burials have been found beneath many Andean pyramid platforms, as here at Moche El Brujo.

Above: Early Intermediate Period Moche lords were elaborately buried in richly furnished tombs, only a few of which remain unlooted.

Lord of Sipán' and in the topmost level were the tombs of the 'Lord of Sipán' and of the Owl Priest. The levels of tombs contain burials, artefacts and depicted scenes that confirm the ritual scene images on the walls, ceramics, textiles and metalwork excavated at other Moche sites, especially the ritual sacrificial scenes painted on red-on-white ceramics and on murals. The Sipán tombs date from *c.*AD100–300. The offerings in the tombs and the costumes worn by the deceased are identical to those worn by the priests depicted in the sacrificial ceremonies.

LORDS OF SIPÁN AND OWL PRIEST

The principal body in Tomb 1, of the 'Lord of Sipán' – undoubtedly that of a local noble or regional ruler of the Lambayeque Valley – personified the Warrior Priest. He wore a crescent-shaped back-flap and

Right: Moche elite deceased were richly dressed and their faces covered with sheet-gold masks. This example has copper inlaid eyes and traces of red paint.

rattles suspended from his belt. Both back-flap and rattles are decorated with the image of the Decapitator God, in this case a human-like spider with a characteristic Decapitator fanged mouth and double ear-ornaments, perched on a golden web. The spider imagery is thought to reflect the parallel of the blood-letting of sacrificial victims and the spider's sucking of the life juices of its prey.

Offerings consisted of three pairs of gold and turquoise ear-spools (one of which shows a Moche warrior in full armour); a gold, crescent-shaped head-dress; a crescent-shaped nose-ornament; and one gold and one silver *tumi* knife. At the Warrior Priest's side lay a box-like sceptre of gold, embossed with combat scenes, with a spatula-like handle of silver studded with military trappings.

Near Tomb 1, Tomb 2 contained offerings not quite so rich, but significantly including the body of a noble with a gilded copper headdress decorated with

an owl with outspread wings – clearly the Owl or Bird Priest of Moche friezes. Sealed rectangular rooms near the two tombs contained other rich offerings – ceramic vessels and miniature war gear, a headdress, copper goblets – and, even more tellingly, the skeletal remains of severed human hands and feet, probably those of sacrificed victims.

In the lowest levels, Tomb 3 contained the body of the 'Old Lord of Sipán', who lived about five generations earlier. His burial goods included two sceptres – one gold, one silver – and he wore six necklaces – three of gold and three of silver.

PRIESTESS FIGURES

Futher rich tombs confirming the accuracy of the Moche friezes and ceramic scenes come from San José de Moro in the Jequetepeque Valley. Here Christopher Donnan excavated the tombs of two women, which contained silver-alloyed copper headdresses with plume-like tassels, and other trappings of the priestess figure. These tombs have been dated to *c.*AD500–600.

Left: Repoussé-decorated sheet-gold kero *drinking cups from a rich Chimú burial. The one on the right shows warriors or possibly the ancient Chavín Staff Deity.*

ELITE BURIAL, SICÁN STYLE

The Sicán culture, which succeeded the Moche in the Lambayeque Valley, has produced equally rich tomb burials at Batán Grande, a few kilometres (miles) across the valley. Batán Grande was the largest Middle Horizon–Early Intermediate Period religious centre of the Sicán culture in the Lambayeque Valley. The ceremonial precinct comprised 17 adobe brick temple mounds, surrounded by shaft tombs and multi-roomed enclosures, with rich burials and rich furnishings reminiscent of the Moche Sipán lords' burial.

In the 1980s Izumi Shimada excavated the tomb of a Sicán lord at Huca Loro, one of the Batán Grande temple mounds, dated *c.*AD1000. The burial was of a man about 40–50 years old, accompanied by two young women and two children who had probably been sacrificed to accompany him. The lord was buried seated and his head was detached and turned 180 degrees, and tilted back to face upwards. He wore a gold mask and his body was painted with cinnabar. The grave contained vast numbers of objects – most of them gold, silver, or amalgamated precious metals (*tumbaga*) – arranged in caches and containers. The lord's mantle alone was sewn with nearly 2,000 gold foil squares. Other objects included a wooden staff with gold decoration, a gold ceremonial *tumi* knife, a gold headdress, gold shin covers, *tumbaga* gloves, gold ear-spools and a large pile of beads.

RITUAL SACRIFICE

Human and animal sacrifice was a common practice throughout ancient Andean civilization. It became a part of ritual from the Preceramic Period and continued into Inca times. Llama sacrifice was especially important in Tiwanaku, Wari and Inca ritual. The latter is an important scene in the Inca state creation myth. The founders sacrificed a llama to Pacha Mama before entering Cuzco. Mama Huaco sliced open the animal's chest, extracting and inflating the lungs with her breath, and carried them into the city alongside Manco Capac and the gold emblem of Inti.

SEVERED HEADS

These are perhaps the most powerful image of ancient Andean human sacrifice, and are a common theme in textile and pottery decoration, murals and architectural sculpture. Severed heads can be seen dangling from the waists of humans and supernatural beings in all ancient Andean cultures. As well as heads, other severed human body parts feature pictorially and in actuality in tombs.

The marching band of warriors on the monumental slabs at the ceremonial complex of Cerro Sechín is interspersed with dismembered bodies, severed heads – singly and in stacks – and naked captives. One warrior has trophy heads hanging from his waistband. One of the three adobe images at Moxeke is thought to represent a giant-sized severed head.

Severed heads form an important theme in the Chavín Cult, used both as trophy heads and as portrayals of shamanic transformation.

In Paracas and Nazca culture the Oculate Being has streaming trophy heads floating from its body at the ends of cords. Trophy heads feature frequently on Paracas and Nazca textiles and pottery. Real severed human heads were placed in Paracas and Nazca burials. There was

Above: A Nazca warrior or priest displaying a fresh trophy head – an integral part of ancient Andean religion.

a Nazca cult that collected caches of the severed and trepanned trophy skulls of sacrificial victims, and many human skulls have been modified to facilitate stringing them on to a cord.

DECAPITATORS

Titicaca Basin Pukará imagery also featured disembodied human heads. Some were trophy heads carried by realistically depicted humans; others accompanied supernatural beings with feline or serpentine attributes, thought, as in the Chavín Cult, to represent shamans undergoing transformation. The Pukará Decapitator sculpture is a seated male figure holding an axe and severed head, and the Pukará ceramic theme known as 'feline man' depicts pairs of fanged men lunging or running, facing one another or one chasing the other, each carrying a

Left: Nazca cemeteries included caches of skulls, many of which show trepanation and perforations for threading on to a cord.

Above: The Moche Pañamarca mural (restoration drawing) depicts the sacrifice ceremony, presided over by a priestess.

severed head and a staff. A cache of human lower jawbones found at Pukará indicates ritual sacrifice and/or warfare, either in the real or mythological world.

Images of the Decapitator God dominated temple and tomb friezes and murals in the Moche capital and are found at Sipán in the Lambayeque Valley, where the tomb of the Lord of Sipán was found. The nearby tomb of the Owl Priest contained boxes of offerings that included the bones of severed human hands and feet. Similar to the Pukará Decapitator, the Moche god holds a crescent-shaped *tumi* ceremonial knife in one hand and a severed human head in the other.

Tiwanaku and Wari craftsmen continued the severed-head theme in all media. The Akapana Temple at Tiwanaku incorporated a buried cache of sacrificed llama bones. Most of the human skeletons found buried on the first terrace and under its foundations were headless, and at the base of the western staircase a black basalt image of a seated, puma-headed

person (*chachapuma*) holding a severed head in his lap was found. Another Tiwanaku *chachapuma* sculpture is a standing figure holding a severed head.

The ultimate severed head is perhaps that of Atahualpa/Inkarrí, who was killed by the Spaniards. His body parts were buried in different parts of the kingdom, with his head in Lima. It is said that one day a new body will grow from his head, and the Inca emperor will return to revive the people's former glory.

SACRIFICIAL BURIALS

Human sacrifice became not only a part of religious ceremonies necessary to honour the gods, but also a ritual associated with elite burial, emphasizing the power and importance of the individual.

The earliest evidence indicative of human sacrifice comes from two burials at Late Preceramic Huaca de los Sacrificios at Aspero. The first was of an adult, tightly flexed with the joints cut to force the unnatural position and to fit the body into a small pit, wrapped only in plain cloth. The second was of a two-month-old infant placed on its right side. It wore a cloth cap and was wrapped in

cotton textile. Accompanying it were a gourd bowl and 500 clay, shell and plant beads. This bundle was placed in a basket, the whole wrapped in another layer of cloth, then rolled in a cane mat and tied with white cotton strips, and finally laid on two cotton wads. The assemblage was covered with an inverted, finely sculptured stone basin. The pair appears to commemorate the premature death of an infant of important lineage and a sacrificial victim to accompany its burial.

The Paracas Cavernas and Nazca Cahuachi cemeteries show numerous signs of ritual human sacrifice. Caches of skulls and trepanning have been mentioned. At Cahuachi it is obvious that some individuals were sacrificial victims. While honoured burials were mummified and accompanied by exquisitely decorated, multicoloured woven burial coats and pottery, sometimes with animal sacrifices, the sacrificial victims – men, women and children – had excrement inserted into the mouth, their skull perforated for threading on to a cord, their eyes blocked, and their mouth pinned by cactus spines or the tongue removed and placed in a pouch.

COMMEMORATIVE SACRIFICES

The roughly contemporary Moche culture of the northern coastal valleys practised a ritual of elite burial through generations as the huge Huaca del Sol pyramid was built in the capital, Cerro Blanco. A burial oriented north–south, as was the pyramid platform, was made near the base of the first phase of construction. Later burials were incorporated in successive phases as the platform was enlarged. There were several burials with mats and textiles within the adobe brick layers of the third phase, some of them of adolescents. Lastly, on top of the final construction stage of the fourth phase was an interment of a man and a woman, extended on their backs, accompanied by 31 globular vessels. The exact meanings of such burials cannot be known, but their association within construction phases of the huge platform was probably as sacrificial offerings for the well-being of the Moche people and their rulers.

Such a conclusion is strengthened by what can only have been a mass sacrifice behind the twin pyramids of Huaca de la Luna, also at Cerro Blanco. An enclosure at the base of the platform contained the mass grave of 40 men, aged 15 to 30, many of them deliberately mutilated. They may have been sacrificed to the gods during a time of

Above: As well as human sacrifice, animal offerings to the gods were a regular ancient Andean religious practice, performed at designated times of the year.

heavy rain caused by an El Niño event to solicit the return of good weather, for the sacrificial victims were covered in a thick layer of water-deposited sediments and the bones showed signs of cutting and of deliberate fracturing. As El Niño events occurred regularly in cycles, there may be other such mass sacrifices yet to be discovered.

The sacrificial scenes on Moche ceramics were actually performed by Moche lords such as the elite individuals known as the Lord of Sipán and the Owl Priest at Sipán. Judging by the frequency with which the scenes are shown on ceramics and murals, the ritual was a regular event, perhaps re-enacting a mythical story. The tradition of sacrifice appears to have survived the collapse of Moche power, even within the Lambayeque Valley, as illustrated in the sacrifice of two women and two children at later Lambayeque-Sicán Huaca Loro (Batán Grande).

CAPACOCHA SACRIFICE

The Incas associated red with conquest and blood. The chronicler Murúa says that each red woollen thread of the Inca

Left: Ritual sacrifice was performed by priests, perhaps impersonating gods or in shamanic 'transformation', as here, wearing a jaguar or puma mask.

state insignia, the Mascaypacha – a crimson tassel hung from a braid tied around the head – represented a conquered people and also the blood of an enemy's severed head.

The Inca practice of *capacocha* sacrifice was a ritual that continued these ancient traditions. As well as honouring the gods, it emphasized the power of the Inca rulers and maintained control over subjugated peoples. Specially selected individuals, usually children, from among the high-ranking *ayllu* kinship lineages of the provinces of the empire were brought to Cuzco to be prepared for the ritual. The selection was made annually and those chosen were destined to be sacrificial victims after ritual ceremonies in the capital. *Capacocha* sacrifices

Right: A Chimú ritual gold tumi *sacrificial knife, for slitting the throat of the victim, decorated with possibly feline heads.*

were offerings to either the sun god Inti or the creator god Viracocha, or to both of the gods. Momentous events such as war, pestilence, famine or other natural disasters could also provoke *capacocha* sacrifices.

In Cuzco, the chosen ones were sanctified by the priests in the Coricancha precinct, who offered the victims to Viracocha, and then marched back to their home provinces along sacred *ceque* routes that linked the provinces to the capital. The victims were sacrificed by being clubbed to death, strangled with a cord, having the throat slit before burial, or by being buried alive in a specially constructed shaft-tomb.

Capacocha sacrifices renewed or reconfirmed the bond between the Inca state and the provincial peoples of the empire, reasserted Inca overlordship and reaffirmed the hierarchy between the Inca centre and the provincial *ayllus*.

CAPACOCHA CHILDREN
Children were sometimes drugged with *chicha* (maize beer) before being sacrificed. Votive offerings usually accompanied the victim in death, such as elaborate clothing, male or female figures of gold, silver, bronze or shell dressed in miniature garments, llama figurines and miniature sets of ceramic containers.

The victims were sometimes carried up and left on high mountaintops regarded as sacred *huacas*, where their bodies would sometimes become preserved in the cold dry conditions that prevailed at such high altitudes. Famous examples include those at Cerro el Plomo in the Chilean Andes, Mount Aconcagua on the Argentinian–Chilean border, Puná Island off the coast of Ecuador, the 'ice maiden' at Mount Ampato and the two girls and a boy sacrificed and buried on Mount Llullaillaco.

Left: A deer sacrifice performed by Death as a skeleton, displayed on a Moche ceramic stirrup-spouted ceremonial vessel.

MUMMIES AND MUMMIFICATION

This preservative treatment of the human body before burial, or even as a state precluding burial, was the ultimate ancient Andean expression of ancestor reverence. It was not an attempt to cheat death on Earth, nor a denial of the cycle of life, but rather an act of recognition of the next stage in the cycle. It was a preparation for the journey and a method of preservation that maintained the contact between those living in this world and those who had moved on to the next stage. In fact, mummification was

not necessarily always achieved deliberately, but could also be the result of climatic conditions, since the desiccating conditions of the desert would preserve exposed bodies. In the same way, desiccation and freeze-drying methods used to preserve stored foodstuffs had been discovered by the ancient Andeans probably accidentally originally, and then deliberately applied.

Above: Cinchorros mummifiction in northern coastal Chile predates Egyptian burials by some 500 years.

THE CHINCHORROS MUMMIES

The earliest mummification in the world was practised by the people of the Chinchorros culture in the Chilean Atacama Desert, starting about 5000BC. The Atacama is one of the bleakest places on Earth and officially recognized as the driest.

Mummification by the Chinchorros predates the earliest Egyptian mummification by about 500 years. It also demonstrates the beginnings of differentiation in burial practices within their community by the special treatment of chosen individuals. Most Chinchorros dead were buried in earthen graves without special treatment. About 250 individuals, however, had been preserved. Curiously these earliest mummies were not of revered elderly members of society; rather the majority of them are of newborns, children or adolescents.

Chinchorros 'morticians' perfected a high degree of skill. The deceased body was left exposed to decompose then completely de-fleshed. Cerebral and visceral matter were extracted and the

Left: Removal of the soft material, salting and careful wrapping helped to preserve organic materials in Paracas burials.

skin treated with salt to help preserve it. The bones were then reassembled as in life and secured in their positions with cords and cane supports. The form of the body was then replaced with fibre, feather and clay stuffing, held inside the skin, which was stitched in sections at the tops of the arms, wrists, torso, abdomen, groin, knees and shins as necessary. A clay death mask was applied to the skull, complete with sculpted and painted facial features, and a coating of clay applied to the body to delineate fingers and toes, with painted finger- and toenails. A wig of human hair was often attached as well. The result was a stiffened, statue-like form.

There is variation in treatment, presumably owing to individual skill and developments in preservation methods over generations.

The mummy was kept above ground as a continuing family member. Some mummies show surface damage, which in some cases was repaired. The preserved cadavers were clearly kept accessible for some time before finally being buried. Some burials were in family groups of adults and children. One such interment spanned three generations from infants and children to mature adults and a few very aged adults.

The inclusion of infants and children, especially separately or in group burials of the young, seems to rule out specific ancestor worship. However, the development of social hierarchy and perhaps lineage privilege is shown by the selection. Presumably special treatment and inclusion above ground within the community continued until the lineage no longer merited a distinct social position, at which time the mummy was then buried in an earthen grave.

LA PALOMA

The Chinchorros mummies were not the only ancient Andean attempts to preserve the body after death. The Preceramic site of La Paloma on the central Peruvian

coast in the Mala Valley was short-lived, but comprised three superimposed settlements with some 4,000 to 5,000 circular huts in total. Abandoned huts later served as graves in which, from as early as about 4000BC, corpses were treated with salt to deter putrefaction. In combination with the dry coastal desert climate, the bodies were desiccated and stiffened as whole forms. At the time, such treatment contrasted sharply with the burial of disarticulated bodies in tropical and other areas.

THE ESSENCE OF PRESERVATION

Even these earliest methods of mummification seem to recognize the concept of essence. The methods do not attempt to halt decomposition of the flesh. Rather

Above: A richly coloured Paracas woollen burial wrap, decorated with felines and perhaps the face of the Oculate Being, reveals the high status of a burial.

they preserve the essence of the earthly form, presumably in order to provide a 'vessel' for the journey of the spirit, or 'vital force', that ancient Andeans believed to be the next stage in the cycle of life. In Inca times, mummies were the preferred symbol of corporate identity and kinship solidarity. The Chinchorros and La Paloma peoples' early efforts at mummification reveal the antiquity of Andean belief that an intact body vessel was critical for the spirit to be able to enter the afterlife and join the world of the ancestors.

The elite burials of the north-coast Moche Sipán lords and later Sicán lords in the Lambayeque Valley were not deliberately mummified. The tradition of elaborate trappings certainly prevailed, but there was no deliberate mummification of the bodies. Their exquisite garments and tomb furniture did not, in the long term, preserve the bodies of the deceased lords, but their dress and grave goods certainly reveal a desire to prepare them and supply them for their journeys into the afterlife.

THE PARACAS/NAZCA MUMMIES

The traditions and concepts established at Chinchorros and La Paloma continued at Early Horizon Paracas and Early Intermediate Period Nazca, about halfway along the coast between the two Preceramic sites. The elaborate mummy bundles interred in the three Paracas

Below: Richly dyed multiple layers of cotton and woollen burial textiles and a feathered headdress emphasize the importance of this Paracas individual.

cemeteries – Cavernas, Cabeza Larga and Necropolis – and the Nazca Cahuachi cemetery show a multi-layered established social hierarchy, clearly defined by the levels of treatment in burial. The dry desert climate was a significant element in preservation, while the elaborate treatment of Paracas and Nazca corpses in multiple layers of burial textiles protected the mummies from deterioration. Social position was indicated by the size and elaboration of the mummy bundle. Once again, the treatment was to provide a vessel for the journey into the afterlife.

The attention to detail in procedures and the multiple layers of textiles and other trappings in Paracas and Nazca burials have been described above. The importation of foreign objects and materials in Paracas and Nazca graves – including exotic shells and llama wool garments, as well as the native-grown cotton textiles – reveals the extent of contact and trade between the coast and other regions, both sierra and tropical. It is significant that with such long-distance communication must have come ideas as well as objects and commodities, and it is this factor that perpetuated the Andean concepts of mummification and concepts about the nature of the afterlife. The time and labour required to produce one Paracas elite mummy bundle demonstrates the depth and sincerity of these beliefs.

The Pre-Inca practice of mummification is emphasized by the

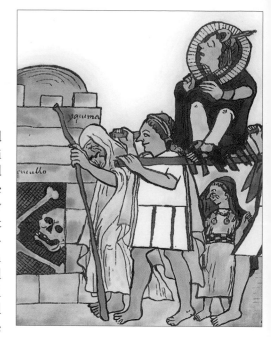

Above: An Inca mummy bundle borne on a litter for deposit in a mausoleum, from which it could be brought out on ritual occasions.

discovery of a row of mummy bundles in the burial of the puma-headed priest (*chachapuma*) beneath the summit structures of the Akapana platform at Tiwanaku. The priestly mummy's importance was accentuated by a row of mummies facing him in the tomb.

CHIMÚ/INCA MUMMIFICATION

Late Intermediate Period Chimú and Late Horizon Inca mummification was the culmination of the long tradition of Andean preservation of the body for the afterlife. Chimú and Inca mummification was achieved in a manner essentially the same as the methods developed by the Paracas people, the critical elements being desiccation and an elaborate mummy bundle of textiles and elaborate garments and jewellery, including precious metals and exotic items. Embalming included the use of alcohol – *chicha* beer made from the maize cultivated in a field near Cuzco was produced expressly to embalm the body of the ancestor Mama Huaco and was used for the succeeding Inca Qoya empresses.

INCA *MALLQUIS* MUMMIES

Every Inca community would have had its special *mallqui* (as it was called in the central and northern Andes) or *munao* (as it was called along the central coast).

The *mallqui* mummy was the community-level founding ancestor, the protohuman descendant of the deities – the great *huacas* such as Inti (the sun) or Illapa (thunder and lightning). In time, the term was applied to more recent ancestors of the kin group. Alongside *mallquis*, ancestors could also be 'mummified' in a transformed state: ancestors who had been petrified and who stood in sacred locations around the landscape. These were known as *huancas*, *chacrayocs* and *marcayocs*. Like the *mallquis*, these stone ancestors represented the first occupation of the region and the first *ayllu* kinship group called out by Con Tici, Imaymana or Tocapo Viracocha at the time of creation.

Inca *mallquis* were commonly kept in caves or in special rooms near the community. Some caves were reported by Spanish priests to hold hundreds of mummified ancestors. The Inca royal mummies – both the Sapa Inca (Inti) and the empress Qoya (Quilla) – were housed in special rooms in the Coricancha Temple in Cuzco, to be brought out on auspicious occasions and festivals and included as 'living' members of the royal household. After the Spanish Conquest they survived, hidden by Incas reluctant to relinquish ancient beliefs, until the late 16th century, when Spanish priests and administrators finally tracked them down and burned them as heretical.

CHIMÚ ROYAL MUMMIES

The immense Chimú capital at Chan Chan in the Moche Valley had at its core the walled city of *ciudadellas*, which housed the living and dead royal households of the Chimú kings. Each *ciudadella* compound comprised a 'city within the city' to accommodate the mummified remains of the king and both dead and living retainers. They 'lived' in rooms on special platforms, including labyrinthine divisions and thousands of storerooms and niches, and even miniature U-shaped ceremonial structures harking back to the most ancient cultures of the north coast.

FREEZE-DRIED MUMMIES

Another type of mummification occurred, perhaps intentionally, in the desiccated climatic condition of remote mountaintops. These were the *capacocha* child and young adult victims of the Inca ritual sacrifice of chosen representatives from the provinces of the empire. Cold storage of sierra agricultural production was a long-standing practice, complementing the

Above: A Middle Horizon Wari mummy bundle. They were preserved and brought out on special occasions by most Andean cultures from the Early Horizon onward.

hot, dry conditions used to dry foods by desert cultures. In the remote, dry, cold high-sierra locations of *capacocha* sacrifice and burial, the combination of elaborate bundling in textiles and the climatic conditions naturally preserved the bodies. The locations and the intent to revisit the *huacas* thus created by the sacrifice indicates that preservation through mummification was counted upon.

ANCESTOR WORSHIP

Reverence for one's *ayllu* kinship ancestors was integral in Inca society regardless of social rank. Special veneration was given to nobles and supreme respect to the royal pair. The enshrined mummies of the Incas and their Qoya wives were carefully tended. Even today the skull of an ancestor is kept in some Andean households to 'watch over' it and its occupants.

Signs of pre-Inca ancestor reverence are evident in the elaborate preparation and care of bodies in Paracas and Nazca cemeteries; especially revealing is the continued reopening of tombs to inter new family members or the maintenance of access to *chullpa* towers for the same purpose. Like so many practices in Andean civilization, the intensity of

ancestor worship reached its most vivid and demonstrative phase among the Incas, who, with the Chimú, developed substantial industries around ancestor worship.

THE ROLE OF *MALLQUIS*

The mummified remains (*mallquis*) of Chimú and Inca rulers and their queens were cared for by dedicated cults. At Chan Chan they were housed in the *ciudadella* compounds. The cults of Inti and Quilla were housed in the Coricancha precinct in Cuzco. The *acllas* (chosen women) of Inti not only tended the *mallquis* of former Sapa Incas but were also the concubines of the reigning Sapa, thus forming a worldly link between the ancestors and the living Inti.

Every *ayllu* maintained mummified ancestor bundles and housed them carefully in special buildings or in nearby caves. *Mallquis* were believed to be the repositories of supernatural powers. As founding ancestors they were regarded as revered divinities, or representatives of the gods, and infused with *camaquen* – the vital force of all living things. They were able to transfer *camaquen* to crops to make them grow and to llama herds to make them multiply. Legendary exploits of *mallquis* were told about their ability to sustain agricultural production. They were responsible for the introduction of the different regional crops and for maintaining the fertility of the land. They had taught the people the different methods of agriculture such as irrigation and terracing to increase production.

Such beliefs maintained established land rights and the mutual obligations within and between *ayllu* kinship groups. They helped to co-ordinate labour between groups, communities and regions.

CONSULTING THE FOREBEARS

Inca ancestor mummies were consulted for numerous reasons, both for everyday concerns and on ceremonial occasions on issues of vital importance. They were consulted before undertaking a journey outside the community, for naming and marriage ceremonies in the life cycle, and on auspicious dates in the agricultural calendar such as sowing and harvesting.

On these occasions they were brought out to participate in the ceremony. They were dressed in fresh clothing, offered food and drink, and generally treated as living, active members of the community. Songs and dances were performed before them and the stories of their exploits told.

Left: An Inca carved wooden head with shell inlay eyes, dressed in dyed textiles – probably from a mummy bundle or more probably a huauque *double.*

Right: Ancestor worship began as early as the Nazca, who placed generations of the deceased in mausoleums and had kinship areas at ritual sites such as Cahuachi.

Spanish attempts to eradicate what they regarded as idolatrous beliefs were fiercely and secretively resisted. Local-level ancestors were considered crucial to community coherence, and most survived well into the 17th century.

HUAUQUES

The Quechua word *huauque* means 'brother'. The term was especially applied to man-made doubles – statues made in the images of the ruling Sapa Incas and other chiefs and nobles during their lifetimes. In his *Historia del Nuevo Mundo*, Bernabé Cobo describes these effigies as well dressed and of various sizes, and says that they were held equivalent to the imperial and noble *mallquis*. They included hollows wherein parts of the reigning emperor were placed when he

Below: As the Incas were so attached to their mummies and ancestor worship, here depicted by an ancestor mummy on a litter, it took the Spaniards over a century to stamp it out.

was alive, such as trimmings from his hair or fingernails. Upon his death the ashes of his burned viscera were usually put into the hollow. Many such duplicates were hunted down by the Spaniards and destroyed along with the actual mummies.

Huauques were made of different materials and had more refined characteristics according to rank. The *huauque* of the upper division of an *ayllu* would have proper facial and other human-like features. That of the lower division would have amorphous or animal features. The *huauques* of earlier Sapa Incas were made of stone while those of the later rulers were made of gold.

After the Sapa Inca's death his royal *panaca* corporation undertook the care of his *mallqui* and *huauque*. During another emperor's lifetime such statues could be used as *mallqui* substitutes, especially on occasions when the real

mummy might be at risk of damage, such as on a long journey or when the living emperor was on a campaign of conquest. The loss of such an idol would be less serious than the actual destruction of a *mallqui*, for loss of the latter would amount to a state disaster: it would mean the loss of the *panaca's* identity.

A *huauque* could also represent a mythical ancestor. In this case invented descent could be confirmed by the effigy for political expediency. Once again, Inca practice appears to follow ancient Andean traditions. The greenstone idol Yampallec of the Sicán ruler Naymlap accompanied him in his conquest of the Lambayeque Valley, and the attempt of his descendant Fempellec to remove the idol was fiercely and successfully resisted by the priests who constituted the royal *panaca*. Nevertheless, the dynasty ended with Fempellec when the priests disposed of him.

TRANCES AND TRANSFORMATION

The ancient Andean cycle of life included trances and transformations during which life on earth was left and other worlds or states of being were entered.

TRANSFORMATIONAL STATES

Some temporary states of being could be experienced by everyone: for example near-death conditions, deep sleep, fainting and drunkenness. More profound states, such as transformation in order to commune with the spirit world, however, were usually drug-induced and were the realm of the shamans and high priests.

Below: This Moche effigy vessel depicts a jaguar-attired shaman with a jaguar emerging from his head.

That such beliefs, like most Andean religious concepts, were ancient is shown in the series of transformation sculptures at Chavín de Huántar in the circular sunken court of the New Temple. These portray a classic trip – the transformation of a human shaman into a revered jaguar. During such a transformation the shaman acquired the powers and wisdom of the animal into which he or she was changed.

Other states of transformation included the conversion of animals and of human heroes or deities into stone, to become sacred regional *huacas*. The reverse could also happen: stones or other features of the landscape could temporarily transform into living beings. The classic example is the calling upon the gods by Pachacuti Inca Yupanqui for help against the Chanca assault on Cuzco, traditionally in 1438. The gods transformed the stones of Pururaucas field into warriors. After the defeat of the Chancas, Pachacuti ordered that the stones should be gathered and distributed among the capital's shrines.

The Moche mural known as the 'Revolt of the Objects' represents another transformational theme – that of everyday objects sprouting limbs and humans with animal heads. This mythical story of the world gone mad and then returned to order was still told in Inca times and recorded by the Spaniards.

SHAMANSIM

This is the term used to describe a person who has special powers, usually aided by hallucinatory plant drugs, to gain access to the spirit world. In ancient Andean cultures the role of the shaman was crucial in everyday life. Priests of the most important temples, including the retainers of the most important oracles and shrines, such as Chavín de Huántar, Pachacamac and the

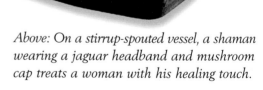

Above: On a stirrup-spouted vessel, a shaman wearing a jaguar headband and mushroom cap treats a woman with his healing touch.

Island of the Sun, were supreme shamans, but every local community would have had their local shaman as well. While the high priests served as intermediaries between the community and the lofty world of the gods, local shamans were consulted for everyday issues such as sickness and fortune.

Shamans in transformational states or in drug-induced states of being have been depicted in Andean cultures from the time of the building of the earliest dedicated ceremonial precincts. Such duality

*Above: The San Pedro cactus (*Trichocereus pachanoi*) was, and is, a rich source of vision-producing mescaline.*

in being is perhaps expressed in the symbolic crossed-hands friezes of the temple walls at Preceramic Period Kotosh. At the Initial Period coastal sites of Garagay, human–animal transformation is depicted in images of insects with human heads, and at Moxeke the earliest representation of shamanic trance may be represented by the adobe sculptures. Spiders with human heads, frequently depicted in the Moche and other cultures, were symbolic as predictors of the future, especially on climatic matters. Moche effigy pots even depict scenes of shamans at work, bent over their patients lying prone before them.

Below: A northern Moche ceramic figurine from the Vicus region shows a shaman clearly in a trance, sporting enhanced feline canines.

The role-taking of humans as deities in scenes of ritual is most famously depicted in the sacrificial scenes on Moche pottery and murals showing the Warrior Priest, Owl Priest and a priestess re-enacting the blood-letting ritual after symbolic combat.

HALLUCINOGENS

Shamanic transformation and trance for curative or special powers was normally induced through the use of hallucinatory plant drugs. The most common hallucinogens were coca leaves (*Erythroxylon coca*), coca incense, the San Pedro cactus (*Trichocereus pachanoi*) (the source of vision-producing mescaline), tobacco and various tropical mushrooms.

Classic characteristics of a hallucinogenic trance are shown in the adobe sculptures of Moxeke and Huaca de los Reyes: jawless lower mouth and/or fangs, flared nostrils and wide eyes with pendent irises. Such symbolic imagery is prolific in Chavín art and widely distributed in the northern and central Andean and coastal regions, and farther south at Karwa (Paracas). Drug-induced stares were woven into the faces of Paracas and Nazca fabrics and on pottery decoration. The faces of countless Moche ceramic effigy vessels and figures in ceramic and mural story scenes reveal otherworldly states of being.

In addition to depictions of various hallucinogenic states, there was a variety of drug paraphernalia, including snuff trays, tubes, pipes and small

knives for chopping. Coca leaves were chewed in a complex, many-staged ritual connected to war and sacrifice. Coca was also frequently used, along with *chicha* beer, to drug sacrificial victims before dispatching them.

Drug paraphernalia has frequently been found among grave goods, but a unique cave burial of a local medicine man, herbalist or shaman of the Callahuaya people, dated to the latter half of the 5th century AD, was found near Huari. He was accompanied by the tools of his practice: a wooden snuff tablet decorated with a Tiwanaku 'attendant angel' figure with a trophy head on its chest; a basket with multi-coloured front-facing deity figures; and various herbal plants that would have been used in his trade.

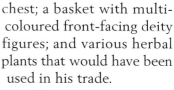

Left: The Moche often displayed shamanic healing rituals in their ceramics. Here a shaman wearing a feline headband prays, probably to the gods, on behalf of a sick or dead person.

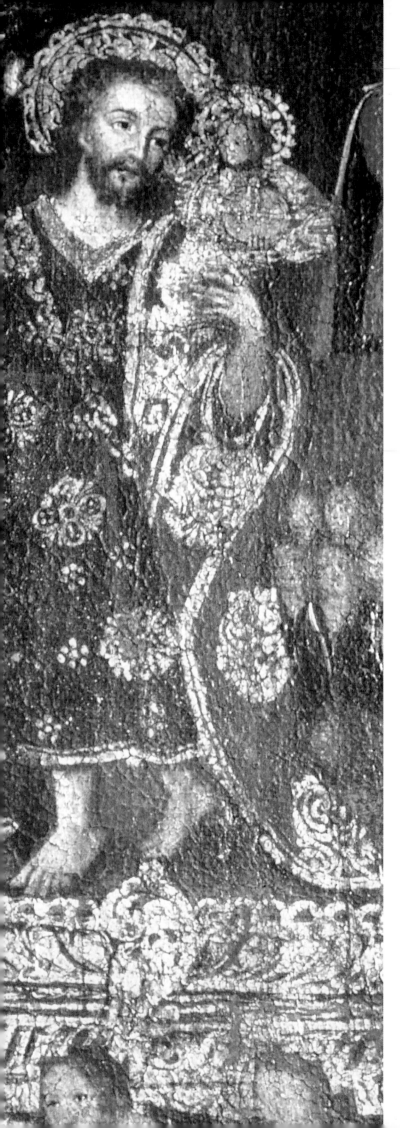

CHAPTER SIX

A NEW GOD

Conversion of the peoples of Mesoamerica and South America began shortly after Columbus landed on the islands of the Caribbean Sea. Once it was realized that he had not sailed west and reached the Orient, the Christian kings and queens of Spain and Portugal and their clergy saw a ripe new world for conversion to the path of Christ.

Many concepts in Christianity – in this case Spanish Catholicism – were ideas not unfamiliar, superficially, to ancient Andean beliefs. Similarly, Christian priests interpreted various elements in the mythical stories related to them by their converts as aspects of or vague references to Judeo-Christian truth.

Native Andeans were selective in their adoption of Spanish customs and tried to maintain as many of their cherished beliefs as they could. They were accustomed to having foreign gods forced upon them and to incorporating them into their pantheon, for the Incas had been as energetic as the Spaniards in this practice.

Andeans interpreted Christianity in their own way, blending it into their own beliefs, and adapting to incorporate the new 'faith'. The outcome was an 'Andean Catholicism' that persists to the present day. In this way Andeans are 'dual citizens' in the worlds of the past and the present.

Despite great changes in Andean culture during the 500 years after the Spanish Conquest, much of Andean life remains inspired by the ancient concepts of exchange, collectivity, transformation and essence.

Left: An 18th-century Spanish colonial Corpus Christi procession. The bearing of the figure on a litter may be a vestige of Inca ancestor worship.

THE MEETING OF TWO GREAT FAITHS

When the Incas were expanding their empire, they had insisted that the state cult of Inti become part of the religion of their subjects. However, ancient Andean religious belief had always had many gods, not just one: there was an overarching creator god (with several regional names), but also many local gods. Belief in the entire landscape as sacred could not deny the relevance of local gods in the development of pre-Inca cultures. So the Incas tried to incorporate all these gods into their cult rather than to exclude them, and to show that the ancient ways and legends were, in fact, part of their own inheritance, and that they were merely the final arbiters.

When their fortunes changed with the arrival of Francisco Pizarro, however, it was the turn of the Incas to be converted. Attempts to convert them and their subject peoples began with Father Valverde, the friar who accompanied Francisco Pizarro

Below: This engraving fancifully depicts an offering to Inti, the Inca sun god. The kneeling man may represent a Catholic priest.

on his expedition against Atahualpa. Feigning peace, Pizarro had instructed Valverde to approach Atahualpa brandishing a crucifix and a Bible as they entered the main courtyard of Cajamarca on 15 November 1532. Valverde delivered a speech on Christianity. His words, translated by an interpreter, were said to be understood by Atahualpa, though we can never be sure. Atahualpa certainly understood what he was being asked to do – forsake his own god for another – for when Valverde handed him the Bible he threw it to the ground and replied, pointing at the sun, 'My god still lives.' This declaration refers to the cult of the Sapa Inca, who, as representative and son of Inti, the sun, was worshipped as a deity.

THE CULT OF VIRACOCHA

Before the Inca state cult transferred its focus to the sun god Inti, Viracocha had been the centre of attention and worship. Yet the antiquity and history of the cult of Viracocha is open to debate. What seems clear is that the Inca Viracocha was a combination of elements. The legend of

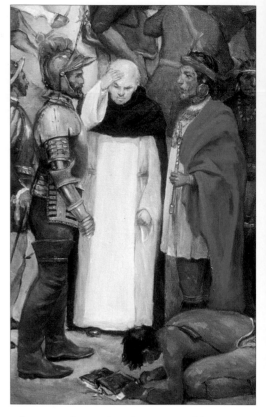

Above: Father Valverde, presumably appalled, had his Bible defiled when Atahualpa allegedly threw it to the ground.

his wanderings gives him the full names of Con Tici (Ticci, Titi or Ticsi) Viracocha Pachayachachic, or Coniraya Viracocha, sometimes including Illya. *Con* was the name of a central coastal creator deity. *Tici* is foundation, beginning or cause. *Ticsi* refers to crystal, *illya* to light. *Pacha* is an element in another coastal creator god, Pachacamac, meaning the universe, time and space. Finally, *yachachic* means teacher.

Viracocha's temple in Cuzco was at Quishuarcancha. Father Bernabé Cobo records that it contained a golden statue of him in human form about the size of a 10-year-old boy. Another Viracocha image was made of textiles and kept in the Temple of the Sun in the Coricancha.

The rise to dominance of Inti over Viracocha occurred during the 15th century, when there was a power struggle in Cuzco. The dispute was between the Inca

Above: The Spaniards symbolically built the Church of Santo Domingo on the foundations of the Inca sacred Coricancha.

ruler Viracocha (and his chosen heir Inca Urco) and Inca Pachacuti, another of his sons. The history was about 100 years old when Pizarro arrived, and details were obscured by time and by the Incas' obsession with having an official version for the new ruler. However, it cannot be coincidental that Viracocha had the name of the deity ultimately to be displac ed and that his supplanter's name was the Quechua word for the revolution of the cycle of time! It was Pachacuti Inca Yupanqui who initiated the installation of the sun cult of Inti and began the rebuilding of Cuzco, the Coricancha Temple and the great Sun Temple of Sacsahuaman.

Among ordinary people the cult of Viracocha was not nearly so prominent as the worship of local deities, especially mountain deities and the earth deity Pacha Mama. The original derivation of *vira* and *cocha* can be traced to Aymara in the Titicaca Basin. In fact, Viracocha became a term used to refer to Spaniards and Christians in general and today is an honorific name for Westerners.

JESUS THE SUN

The Andean equation of Jesus Christ with the sun began in the early colonial period, an association that conformed to their 'former' belief that the Sapa Inca was the son of the sun and their association of Viracocha, creator of the sun and the moon, with Inti. The Christian god and the sun were both celestial deities and their conceptualization was similar.

The sun cult was revived in the 20th century. Today the sun is addressed as Huayna Capac (Young Lord), Hesu Kristu (Jesus Christ), Inti Tayta (Father Sun) and Taytacha (also Jesus Christ), a perfect combination of celestial deity, sun, and father and son.

The equation of the Virgin Mary with Pacha Mama is also colonial. Mary is linked to the moon through the moon's intimate association with the earth and its annual cycles through the agricultural year. The association is most prominent in August, at crop planting. In September the ritual of Coya Raymi (the empress's feast) is held to celebrate its successful completion. The moon is addressed as Mama Quilla (Mother Moon). Women take the active role and issue invitations to men to participate. Women's interest in the crops continues to the December solstice, when young boys take over care of the growing crops and the festival of Capac Raymi is held in honour of the sun.

SHARED BELIEFS

Christian missionaries saw elements in Inca belief that convinced them that they were merely 'lost children' of Christ. Indeed, many Andean religious concepts and Christian beliefs are superficially similar. The Andean concept of dualism – oneness within two – is not unlike the Judeo-Christian trinitarian belief of one within three.

The ultimate creator god Viracocha was a rather remote, overarching deity whose omnipresence was similar to the concept of God the Father. Viracocha's pervading presence throughout the universe was an omnipresent force, not an idol (although, like Christ, he was represented on Earth). Inca stories of a flood and of a single man and woman as progenitors of the human race could be perceived as the essence of Christian truth, if slightly corrupted by the passage of time and errors in record.

The biblical story of creation, in which humans began on earth with a man and a woman created by the supreme deity, resembled Andean belief, which also included a flood that destroyed everything that went before. Plagues and divine retribution were familiar, and sacrifices and gifts to the gods – for example the mass sacrifice at Huaca de la Luna at

Below: In this version of Father Valverde's attempt to convert Atahualpa, Pizarro is depicted kneeling – an unlikely occurrence.

Cerro Blanco to alleviate the effects of an El Niño event – were familiar pleas to the supreme being for help in bearing life's daily burdens.

Similarly, the legend of the wandering beggar Viracocha – as Christ, Son of God, who walked upon the earth and taught the people – was reconciled and incorporated. The ability of Viracocha to walk on water convinced many that Jesus must have come to the New World, perhaps after his resurrection or in a second visitation.

Sacred places of worship were also a familiar idea, including wells, springs and the importance of water. The concept of pilgrimage to sacred sites had been an Andean practice from at least the Early Horizon Chavín Cult. Sacred places as repositories for relics were everywhere in the Andean countryside and in villages, towns and cities. Christian worship and attribution of miraculous powers to saints' bones and pieces of the cross was recognizable.

FAMILIAR BELIEFS

Saints' feast days are celebrated with dances, the performers wearing masks to impersonate saints, much as the ancient Moche blood-sacrifice figures wore deity masks. A stone statue of Viracocha made by the Canas peoples of Cacha in the image of a Spanish priest in long white robes, and Viracocha's calling out of the ancestors, were attributed to the Titicaca Basin deity Tunapa, whom the native chronicler Pachacuti Yamqui believed to be Saint Thomas. Another native chronicler, Guamon Poma, believed Viracocha was Saint Bartholomew.

SHARED SYMBOLS

Ancient Andeans were also comfortable with much of Christian symbolism. Worship involved sacred objects: the cross, the chalice, candles and sacred vestments. The creed was 'kept' and recorded in the Bible. God was the creator and his

son was Jesus, who walked the earth and taught. Drugs were used: incense and wine in ceremony and sacred acts. And there was sacrifice, the crucifixion of Jesus Christ, a concept definitely familiar to ancient Andeans.

FINDING COMMON GROUND

Like the Incas, Christian preachers were willing to 'bend' a little in their efforts to convince themselves that their New World

Above: Ancient Andeans would have recognized the concept of human sacrifice but have had difficulty with the victim being described as the god himself.

converts' beliefs proved that Christian religion had been witnessed throughout the world – that things were always as they were in their Christian world. However, the recorders were the Spaniards themselves, and they were inclined to alter the stories they were told to fit preconceived ideas. For example, the three Viracochas (Con Tici, Imaymana and Tocapo) were a perfect triad that could be equated with the Holy Trinity, but what sixteenth-century Spanish priests did not know was that triadism is a concept in many cultures in the world.

In Andean triadism the kin-relationship of father and two sons, or three brothers, is less important than the structure of one principal and two helpers. This form is present in cult histories throughout the Andes. In some versions there is a fourth figure, Taguapaca, who disobeyed the father's instructions and was thrown into the River Desaguadero for his disobedience – the perfect foil of evil destroyed to leave the three principals of the narrative.

One of the ways in which Andean belief has survived is by being combined with Christianity. Some combinations were

Below: This puma devouring sinners was an attempt to seduce Native Americans into Christian belief using an Andean symbol.

Right: The Virgin Mary here remarkably resembles an Inca mummy bundle, and even has a staff-holding Inca depicted on her gown.

deliberate, as Spanish priests tried to ease the acceptance of Christianity. Much else was a natural blending of the Andeans' own beliefs with Christian ones: for example the sun is merged with Jesus, the Virgin Mary with Pacha Mama (the earth goddess) and Saint James of Santiago with Illapa.

IMPORTANT DIFFERENCES

Belief in an afterlife is a universal religious concept, though the idea that one's conduct on Earth was partly responsible for the nature of the afterlife was less entrenched in Andean belief. The difference was the Andean concept of *pachacuti*: a great cycle that repeated endlessly through time. Suffering was here on Earth, and the final journey of the spirit after physical death was allied to the Andean concept of essence, and the idea that death was the ultimate stage in life's cycle, with no thought of rebirth.

The concept of a second coming was embraced in Inkarrí, but is fundamentally more concerned with the return of the Incas to their rightful place in the scheme of things, their ingrained belief in *pachacuti* and a destiny to rule, rather than the Christian concept of Christ's return.

Spanish priests were unable to suppress the Inca solar cult: it survived in the central highlands and to the coast at Pachacamac. The sun continued to be a principal deity superior to mountain protector-guardian deities, and two aspects were recognized as daytime-sun, in the sky, and night-time sun, which travelled through the earth overnight. Throughout the highlands, the cults of Inti and Punchao (daytime sun) survived into colonial times and were associated with maize and the potato. In the 1560s a messianic movement called Taqui Onqoy (dancing sickness) revived the ancient *huacas* of Titicaca, Pachacamac and others,

perhaps eschewing the sun as associated with the Inca elite, who had been overpowered by the Spaniards.

Ultimately, ancient Andean beliefs could not be reconciled with Christian ones. The connections and parallels were too vague, and there were too many variations in Andean belief. Although there are undoubtedly similarities, they are merely superficial, for the concept of one god was fundamentally alien to ancient Andeans. However, Andeans were happy to keep their ancient religious ideas alongside Christianity, as long as they didn't have to give them up entirely. Thus, the Incas remained true to their belief in an established cycle of life in which they were at the cusp, destined to rule in the name of Inti. They were following the path that was ordained, fulfilling their destiny. Of course, the Spanish conquistadors held a similar belief, but they were conquering in the name of *their* god.

SACRED LOCATIONS

Reverence for sacred locations has never abated in Andean belief. From the powers of mountain gods and Pacha Mama to household deities such as Ekkeko, Andeans believe that offerings to such 'gods' can bring good fortune.

Spanish priests and administrators, focusing on conversion and on the elimination of ancestor cults, only slowly realized the tenacity with which Andean peoples stuck to their essential belief in the sacredness of the local landscape. Such beliefs go back to the foundations of the earliest cultures of the Andes and the first architectural ceremonial centres that mimicked the shapes of the landscape. The destruction of cult objects could not weaken such beliefs.

Andeans continue to regard identifiable stones or rock outcrops near their towns as characters from legendary scenes who have been turned to stone.

The ancient site of Pachacamac is perhaps the most ancient pilgrimage site in use. It persisted in colonial times as a

Below: Tens of thousands of people participate annually in the El Calvario ritual, merging Christian belief and sacred places.

sacred place. The Señor de los Milagros, or Crito Morado, here filled the place of the pre-Hispanic cult. Modern Peruvians visit Pachacamac to make offerings, especially to Pacha Mama.

HOUSEHOLD DEITIES

Ekkeko is a case in point. An Aymara deity dating from the Middle Horizon Tiwanaku culture, he was incorporated into Inca religion. Ekkeko household deity figures persisted through colonial times and are kept in households today to bring good luck. They are offered everything from coca leaves to Coca Cola in asking them to bring the household good fortune. The presence of Ekkeko makes every household a 'sacred place'. The use of such deity figures spread in the 1970s to many countries well beyond the Bolivian Altiplano.

Similarly, Inca stone and metal sculptures of plants and animals were considered repositories of health and powers for well-being. They were placed at *huacas* throughout the land. Today, Andeans keep small stones that either resemble animals or plants or have been carved to do so. Known as *inqa, inqaychu,*

Above: Shrines remained sacred to the Inca. The seated-puma-shaped rock at Qenqo continued to remind the Incas of Viracocha.

conopa or *illa*, they are believed to be gifts from mountain *apus*. Some have been passed down through many generations. Modern versions can be miniature plastic trucks, rubber sandals, cans of drink, money or even passports, and they can be bought at pilgrimage sites before being offered to local deities or saints.

Taking an object that belonged to a deceased important person in one's *ayllu* kinship group to that person's favourite place would invoke the person's memory among his descendants and also enhance the power of the sacred place. The act was not merely repetitious, but was meant to build the kin-group's history and link it through time to the present.

HUACA SHRINES

The royal *panaca* and sacred *huacas* of the Inca emperors were especially important to kin-group history. As part of the cult of the Sapa Inca as Inti's representative on earth, when Tupa Yupanqui died, his son Huana Capac visited the places

Above: The Qoyllur Rit'i ritual, begun after an alleged 18th-century miracle, revives the ancient Andean concept of ritual procession.

his father liked best, especially in Cajamarca, and built shrines at them. One tradition in the history of Inca origins describes Mount Huanacauri as the 'father' of the three founding ancestors, who were turned into stone around Cuzco. Even today, some Andeans regard local *huacas* in their region 'like parents'. Such places were believed to have given rise to their ancestors, and local caves were often where Andeans stored the mummified remains of ancestors until they were destroyed in colonial times by the Spaniards. Substantial evidence for

Below: This Qoyllur Rit'i procession is to the sacred Mt Sinakara, where Mariano herded his llamas and met the mestizo boy.

provincial shrine systems like those around Cuzco – for example colonial records – is sparse, however, and probably awaits discovery by ethnohistorians.

QOYLLUR RIT'I

One of the most celebrated 'modern' festivals involving place is Qoyllur Rit'i in the southern Andes, attended annually by tens of thousands of people. Held during the three weeks leading to the feast of Corpus Christi, the ritual is focused on several sanctuaries around Ocongate. Costumed dancers perform in honour of 'El Señor'.

The ritual is a typical mixture of ancient and Christian beliefs. The object of devotion is an image of Christ that miraculously appeared on a rock: El Señor de Qoyllur Rit'i (Lord of the Snow Star). The ritual began in the late 18th century, when the Catholic authorities replaced an indigenous cult with a Christian shrine. The Catholic Church officially accepted the miraculous appearance of Christ's image.

The ancient cult associated Ocongate as a venue of worship at the transition and regeneration of the new year. The blending of Christian and ancient belief revolves around the miracle in which a young llama herder, Mariano, encountered a mestizo boy on Mount Sinakara. Mariano was cold and hungry and the other boy shared his food. Mariano's herd increased and his father offered him new clothes as a reward. Mariano asked for new clothes for his friend too. He took the mestizo boy's

poncho to market to have it duplicated. The Bishop of Cuzco noted the old poncho's fine material and asked Mariano about the mestizo. Church officials sent to meet him encountered him wearing a white tunic, surrounded by a blinding radiance emanating from a silhouette When one official tried to touch it, he grasped a *tayanka* bush, above which, on a rock, appeared the image of Christ crucified. Mariano fell dead and was buried at the foot of the rock where the image appeared. A chapel was built to house the Tanyaka Cross and Mariano's sepulchre. Christ Tanyaka is believed to have been transformed into the rock, and the Catholic Church later had Christ's image painted on the rock-face.

Below: Husband and wife believers burn incense and make an offering to Pacha Mama in a ceremony in the La Paz Valley.

PROCESSIONS, FESTIVALS AND RITES

Architectural forms and sculptures in mud plaster and stone show that processions, ritual festivals and sacred rites were a part of ancient Andean culture.

ANCIENT PROCESSIONS

Ancient Andeans were intimately familiar with the concept of sacred routes. Cuzco alone had more than 300 sacred shrines along sacred *ceque* routes, ranging from monumental buildings to natural features. So important were processional routes to the Incas that archaeologists project their use to as far back as the Initial Period, suggesting that processions through U-shaped ceremonial precincts proceeded down into and through sunken courts, back out of them, and up on to temple platforms mimicking mountains, to honour earth and sky deities.

The established purpose of the famous Nazca desert lines – geoglyphs – was for ritual processions that followed the course of the lines. Geoglyphs of animals, birds or geometric patterns consist of a single line that never crosses itself. There are also nodes from which lines radiate.

The tradition of *ceque* routes made Christian processional routes, such as the Stations of the Cross, easy to comprehend.

Below: The 'festival' of Inti Raymi, the Inca June/winter solstice, attracts large crowds and is taken seriously to revive ancient Inca pageantry at the shrine of Sacsahuaman.

Left: The Nazca even made clay models of ancient processions, including a central shaman.

Pilgrimage to holy shrines was also a common ancient Andean practice. Similarly, ancient Andean sacrificial practices made recognition of the apparent ritual execution of Christ a familiar concept.

The Qoyllur Rit'i ritual involves processions by two groups representing the warm lands of the north-west (from Paucartambo town) and the colder pasture land of the south-east (from Quispicanchis town). The procession represents ancient Andean regional opposition and mutual exchange, and even linguistic dualism, for the Paucartambos are Quechua speakers while the Quispicanchis speak Aymara.

FEAST DAYS

Just as early Christians in a pagan Europe adapted and combined many feast days and ceremonies into the Christian calendar as their religion spread, so Christian Andeans have equated many ancient Andean ceremonial days to established Christian dates.

The recitation of the myth-histories of founding ancestors in provincial communities was made at annual high points such as planting (Pocoymita) and harvesting (Caruaymita), both of which became associated with Christian holy days. Ancient Andeans began to harvest their various crops in mid-April, and finished the collection and storage of produce by early June. These activities coincided with the disappearance of the Pleiades constellation in the night sky in April and its June reappearance above the horizon. The Pleiades were called *collca* ('storehouse') by the Incas, and ancient Andeans regarded it as the celestial container of the essence of all agricultural produce. With the arrival of Christianity, the movable feast of Corpus Christi soon became equated with the rising of the Pleiades at the same time as the rising of the sun.

Festivals mixing ancient Andean ritual with Christian practice and dates are those of Capac Raymi (December summer solstice) and Inti Raymi (June winter solstice), and the revival of the ritual re-enactment of the founding of Cuzco by Manco Capac, celebrated annually.

Such rituals can be regarded as a rejuvenation of ancient belief and power, which would have been understandable

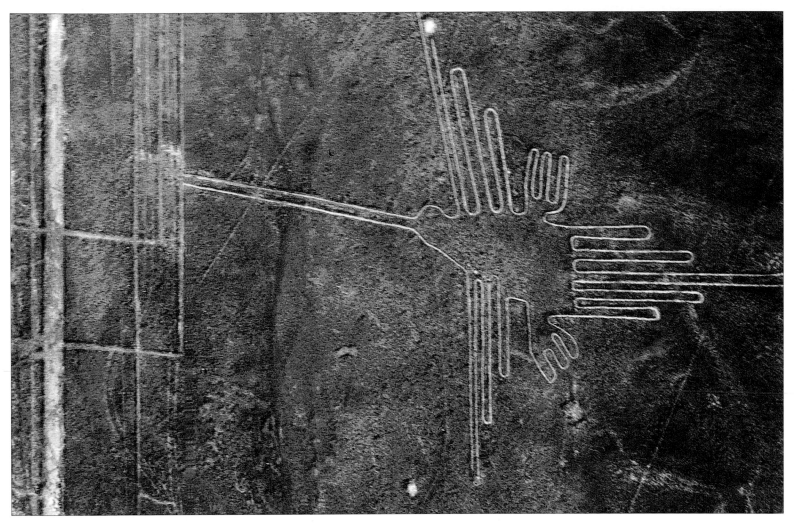

Above: Humming bird in the Nazca desert. Geoglyph lines were thought of as processional pathways, perhaps 'owned' by kin groups.

in an atmosphere and perception of powerlessness against hundreds of years of colonial oppression.

DEEDS OF THE ANCESTORS

When the first Spaniards entered Cuzco they witnessed the arrangement of the mummified Inca emperors in the main plaza. The keepers of Inca history, the *amautas* and *harahuicus*, were responsible for collating the histories and deeds of the emperors. On ritual occasions, it was their task to recite these histories in the forms of short stories by the former and poems by the latter, incorporating stylistic devices such as set speeches, repeated metaphor and refrains intentionally reshaped and elaborated from one performance to the next.

Occasions for such performances included the initiation rites of teenage boys as adults during the month leading up to Capac Raymi (late November–December), the summer solstice. The boys visited the peaks in the southern Cuzco Valley where the Inca ancestors stopped on their route to Cuzco. Other occasions were at the celebration of military victories, royal successions and, of course, royal funerals.

It was Inca Pahcacuti, religious reformer and initiator of the cult of Inti, who ordered that 'songs' (*cantares* in the Spanish chronicles) were sung by the attendants of the imperial 'statues' (ancestor mummies and *huauques*) at 'fiestas'. The performance began with the deeds of Manco Capac, the founder ancestor, and proceeded through the emperors up to the reigning Sapa Inca. Colonial records describe such performances of myth-histories in provincial centres as well.

STAMPING OUT IDOLATRY

Priests and Spanish administrators fought a continuing battle against what they regarded as idolatry, as manifested in the cults and virtual worship of the mummified remains of *ayllu* founders and ancestors. They ruthlessly hunted down and tried the perpetrators of ancestor cults and burned their mummified ancestors, until by the end of the 16th century all were destroyed.

In the eyes of the Incas, the Spaniards were equally wicked in their treatment of Inti. The great golden sun disc that hung in the Coricancha had been awarded to one of the conquistadors, who promptly gambled it away in a late-night card game – thus the Andean expression 'to gamble the sun before dawn'.

REVIVALS

Many Inca rites and processions have been revived, especially in the late 20th century. Based, as were their ancestors, primarily on an agricultural way of life, Native South American descendants and mestizos seek to alleviate the hardships of life by continuing to honour traditional belief in the sacredness of the land of their forefathers and to reconcile this with modern life.

ANIMISM AND COCA

Animism was fundamental in ancient Andean religion: the forces of nature were and are believed to be 'living beings' that affect life. Humans were only one group of beings among animals and plants. The images of supernatural beings based on living animals, such as the jaguar, snakes, predatory birds and spiders, and the depiction of transformation, reveal such belief. Animals were thought to possess powers and wisdom that could benefit humans, and certain humans, the shamans, were capable of shape-shifting to become, temporarily, the animal in question and take on the animal's nature.

Below: This Moche spouted vessel displays an intoxicated shaman, holding his wooden stick and coca container to make coca balls.

THE LIVING EARTH

Agriculture was fundamental to ancient Andean civilization and still forms the basis of most of Andean society. Agricultural fertility is therefore deeply ingrained in the Andean psyche, and with it worship of Pacha Mama – the living earth – and the natural elements. Ceremonial rites to Pacha Mama, the matrix for all life, continue to be performed regularly throughout the year, highlighted on important dates in agriculture, and also when visiting sacred places and at the start of a long journey. At harvest ceremonies, young women impersonate Pacha Mama Suyrumama by wearing long red dresses ('mother earth of the long dress that drags along the ground').

The field called Ayllipampa, near Cuzco, is dedicated to Pacha Mama. Bernabé Cobo described how farmers worshipped her at stone altars containing miniature women's clothing in the middle of the field. Other deities associated with Pachcmama are Mama Oca, Mama Coca and Mama Sara (Maize Mother). Central Andeans continue to maintain that the Inca ancestress Mama Huaco, who sowed the first maize field, and others sustain the agricultural well-being of the community. The field of Sausero outside Cuzco was dedicated to her.

Agricultural ferility is also believed to be affected by mountain *apu* deities and celestial gods, including Illapa (lightning and thunder), Cuichu (rainbow) and Ccoa (a supernatural feline who causes destructive hail).

THE POWER OF *CHICHA*

Today, rural *ayllus* continue to plough and plant communal fields at festivals. There are contests to see who can work fastest at ploughing and planting the largest amount of land. Festive meals are served, accompanied by plenty of *chicha* or maize beer. There are *chicha* libations and offerings of coca to Pacha Mama, the community ancestors and the local

Above: Continuing ancient practice, a modern Peruvian makes an offering of coca leaves to a local deity or saint.

sacred places, alongside Christian prayers to the community's patron saints, who seem to have taken the place of the ancestors.

Llamas are ritually honoured in August. They are force-fed a *chicha*, barley and herbal mash to intoxicate them before being released on to the Altiplano, followed by their equally intoxicated herders singing and playing flutes. Such ritual drunkenness is believed to enhance fertility. Libations are poured to invite Pacha Mama and the *apus* to the celebrations. Intoxication also blurs the distinction between humans, animals and the landscape as they all 'dance together'.

SACRIFICE BEHIND THE ALTAR

Ancient sacrifices and offerings continued in secrecy well into Spanish colonial times. Although known as the 'sacrifice behind the altar' syndrome, this is not

to be taken literally, as the sacrifices and offerings simply occurred in remote places away from churches. Animal sacrifices, together with offerings of agricultural produce and coca, and the burning of incense with prayers are still practised, often alongside offerings of modern 'western' products such as cigarettes and Coca Cola, and also often in connection with Christian ceremonies.

Left: A silver figurine depicts a woman with puffed cheeks, chewing a coca wad, which induces stamina and suppresses hunger.

Mountains (especially volcanoes), caves and springs remain particularly sacred. Mountains continue to be regarded as the dwelling places of the ancestral dead.

The fundamental Andean cosmological frame remains an anchor to Andean society: the sun rises over the sacred mountains in the east, brings life, and sets in the west, the final resting place of the dead.

SHAMANS
Local shamanism also still has an important place in local communities. For everyday illnesses, many Andeans consult their local *curandero*, a person skilled in the use of herbs and potions, harking back to the 5th-century AD Wari cave burial of a herbalist. Shaman-curers were frequently depicted in Moche and other effigy vessels.

Cures include the use of water and perfume exhaled over a (looted) skull from a pre-Hispanic burial, in the belief that the spirit of the deceased person will protect the afflicted as well as the curer from evil interventions. Potent hallucinogenic mescaline brews are still made from the San Pedro cactus. Chants and prayers used in such cures are a mixture

Above: Native South Americans and cholos (people of Spanish descent) in a Christian-native ceremony at El Calvario, Bolivia.

of pre-Hispanic and Christian practices. Sticks, which represent swords, are used to fight with the spirits of 'the other world' and keep them from harming the patient. As in ancient times, the shaman acts as an intermediary between the human and spirit worlds.

COCA
The regular chewing of coca leaves continues as a stimulant and aid in coping with the harsh climate and high Andean altitudes. The Spaniards quickly learned its properties of keeping otherwise exhausted labourers and miners energized, and exploited its perceived sacred symbolic power as, once again, their Christian convictions were compromised by practical needs. Coca cultivation increased under Spanish rule. Coca leaves are a frequent offering to Pacha Mama especially, and there is irony in their 'integration' from ancient use to modern times, for the leaf is referred to as Hostia (the Host) and its ritual consumption compared to Holy Communion.

Coca remains a major part of the Andean indigenous economy and is, of course, exploited internationally in its refinement for the drug trade.

THE RETURN OF THE INCAS

Twentieth-century social studies of Andean culture have discovered an underlying theme that represents a source of post-Conquest cross-Andean unity: the theme of the dying and reviving Inca, as encapsulated in the legend of Inkarrí.

THE FIVE AGES

A late Inca cosmology comprised a five-age sequence of the creation of the Inca world. The First Age was ruled by Viracocha and the other gods, and death was unknown. The Second Age was that of the giants created by Viracocha, who worshipped him but who displeased him and were destroyed by a flood. The Third Age was inhabited by the first humans, again created by Viracocha, but they lived on a primitive level and lacked even the rudiments of civilization. The Fourth Age was that of the *Auca Runa* ('the warriors'), to whom Viracocha presumably imparted the arts of civilization, for these were the creators of the early civilizations such as the Moche and the Tiwanaku.

Below: After unsuccessful revolts against Spanish rule, the legend grew that the Incas retreated east into the rainforest to Paititi.

The Fifth Age was that of the Incas themselves, who spread civilization far and wide through conquest. The Fifth Age ended with the coming of the Spaniards and with the downfall of the Inca Empire, but upon their arrival the Spaniards were hailed as the returning emissaries of the creator and were referred to as *viracochas* – a term still used as one of respect.

THE STORY OF INKARRÍ

Inkarrí is the central character in a post-Spanish Conquest Inca millenarian belief in the 'dying and reviving Inca'. The derivation of the name itself is a combination of the Quechua word *Inca* and the Spanish word *rey*, both meaning 'king' or 'ruler'. The legend foretells a time when the current sufferings of the original peoples of the Andes will be ended in a cataclysmic transformation of the world, in which the Spanish overlords will be destroyed. The true Inca will be resurrected and reinstated in his rightful place as supreme ruler, and prosperity and justice will be returned to the world.

A typical example of one of the versions of the Inkarrí myth recounts how Inkarrí was the son of a savage woman

Above: A modern Peruvian impersonates the Sapa Inca at the festival of Inti Raymi. It is believed that the emperor will one day return.

and Father Sun. Inkarrí was powerful. He harnessed the sun, his father, and the very wind itself. He drove stones with a whip, ordered them around, and founded a city called K'ellk'ata, probably Cuzco. Then he threw a golden rod from a mountaintop, but found that the city did not fit on the plain where it landed, so he moved the city to its present location. When the Spaniards arrived, however, they imprisoned Inkarrí in a secret place, and his head is all that remains. However, Inkarrí is growing a new body and will return when he is whole again.

PACHACUTI

Belief in the return of Inkarrí is clearly in keeping with the Andean concept of *pachacuti*, the revolution or reversal of time and space. It arose from the native populations' sense that the Spaniards had created oppression and injustice. It may hark back to events of the first few

Right: Tupac Amaru, the 'last Inca emperor', was beheaded in Cuzco's central plaza. His head was spirited away and secretly buried.

decades after the Spanish Conquest, in which the last Inca emperor, Atahualpa, was believed to have been beheaded by Francisco Pizarro shortly after his defeat, and to the beheading of Tupac Amaru, a claimant to the Inca throne, who led an unsuccessful revolt against Spanish rule in the 1560s and 1570s. In different accounts, the two heads were taken to Lima or to Cuzco, but in both cases the belief is that, once buried in the ground, the head becomes a seed that rejoins its body in anticipation of return.

THE RETURN TO CUZCO

Another belief concerns the removal of Inca power to a hidden land. The legend records that upon being expelled from Cuzco the Incas travelled east through the mountains. They built bridges as they went, but they placed enchantments on

Below: The retreating Incas built enchanted bridges as they went, so that their route could not be followed.

their route so that no one could follow. If they did, the enchantment caused them to fall asleep on the spot for ever.

The Incas travelled across the mountains into the jungle and established a hidden city called Paititi. Here they remain in hiding. 'Foreigners' who seek Paititi can never find it. One found a talking bridge; when he tried to cross it, he was chased away by huge felines and *amarus* (mythical serpent-dragons) guarding the bridge.

According to the legend, *pachacuti* will turn and the Inca will return, following the route they used when they left Cuzco. There will be tremendous hail and lightning, wind and earthquakes. *Amarus* will roar from mountains and mestizos will be chased away. When the Incas return they will recognize only their *runakuna* descendants, who wear traditional llama-wool clothing, and the Incas will assume their rightful place and rule again.

GLOSSARY

acllas chosen women, picked to serve in the state cult of Inti

acllahuasi special buildings where *acllas* were housed

amarus mythical serpent-dragons

amautas also *harahuicus* Inca record-keepers

andones hillside terraces

apacheta special type of *huaca* – a stone cairn on a mountain pass or at a crossroads

apu sacred deity who lives on a mountain top, or the mountain top itself

aridenes cultivation terraces

atl-atl spear thrower

auca treasonous enemy of the state

audiencias small divisions within Chan Chan *ciudadela*

ayar legendary ancestors of the Incas

ayllu a kinship group or division with mutual obligations to other *ayllus*

ayni the principle that governed cyclicity

capacocha specially selected sacrificial victim

ceque sighting line or sacred pathway leading from Cuzco

chachapuma puma-headed person

chicha beer made from maize

chullpa tower where the Colla people put mummified remains, and into which more could be added

ciudadela Chimú walled compound at Chan Chan

collca storehouse

curaca leader/official

curandero person skilled in the use of herbs and potions

hanan upper

huaca sacred place – a natural, man-made or modified natural feature

huaca adatorio sanctuary or temple

huaca sepultura burial place of the most important deceased individuals

huanca stone(s) regarded as the petrified ancestor of a people or *apu*

huauques man-made statues – doubles – made in the image of the ruling Sapa Incas and other chiefs and nobles during their lifetimes

hurin lower

idolatrías Spanish Colonial documents written as reports of the Spaniards'

investigations of idolatrous practices among the native peoples

inqa (also *inqaychu, conopa* or *illa*) small stones that either resemble animals or plants or have been carved to do so, believed to be gifts from mountain *apus*

intihuatana a 'hitching post of the sun' – special *huaca* of Inti

kalanka rectangular hall used for public functions

kancha residential building

kero a drinking cup, especially for *chicha*, made from wood, pottery, gold or silver

mallquis mummified founding ancestor, Inca emperor or local leader

mama female

mit'a labour service/tax

mitamaes peoples redistributed within an empire

mitamaq the redistribution of people

montaña forested slopes of the Andes

moza commoner/outsider

napa miniature llama figurine

pacarina the place of origin, the place from which one's ancestors (one's tribe, nation or *ayllu* kinship group) emerged

pachacuti a turning over/revolution/a cycle of the world

pampa vast prairie in South America south of the Amazon

panaca kinship group; the royal panaca was the Inca *ayars*

plazas hundidas plazas or sunken courts

puna sierra basin or valley

qhaqha person or animal killed by lightning

quipu system of knotted bundles of string of different colours, used for recording information

quipucamayoqs knot-makers (i.e. makers and keepers of *quipus*)

runakuna Inca descendants who wear traditional llama-wool clothing

runaquipu-camayoc a census recorder

suyu quarter of the Inca Empire

tambo a way-station, which was used to accommodate pilgrims

tocoyrikoq provincial governor

topacusi golden cup or vessel

tumbaga amalgamated precious metals

tumi crescent-shaped knife used for ritual bloodletting or decapitation

wasi covered chamber

yanacona a selected court retainer

yaya male

INDEX